Grandmother Alice

Memoirs from the Home Front
Before Civil War into 1930's

With best wishes –

Reese Hawkins

Presented by her grandson
Reese Hawkins

GRANDMOTHER ALICE

Alice Crain Hawkins
February 23, 1871   June 5, 1937

First Printing 2002

McCleery and Sons Publishing.
3303 Fiechtner Drive SW
Fargo, North Dakota 58103.

All photos from Hawkins Collection.

Author - Reese Hawkins
Author's Assistant - Margaret Hawkins

Cover Photograph of Grandmother Alice 1916
Cover designed by Margaret Hawkins

Publisher - McCleery & Sons Publishing

International Standard Book Number: 1-931916-15-2

*To the memory of
my Grandfather, John L. Hawkins,
and to all his descendants —
many of whom I played with as a child on his farm.*

The wind blows,
shakes a little
as it seeks refuge
in jacket openings.
I lean into it
and warm my hands
in the mittens
Grandma made for me.

There is a light
guiding me on
and when I reach it
it will be my home.

R. H.

FOREWORD

A grandfather remembers his grandmother. A grandmother remembers her ancestors. Both wish they had listened more carefully to family tales when they were children. Still, the grandfather, Reese Hawkins, admits that he remembers hearing his Grandmother Alice tell many of the stories she recorded in her memoirs. If Grandmother Alice forgot some of her ancestors' tales, she also remembered many in great detail. The stories stayed in their memories, waiting to be rediscovered. Some say our lives are shaped by the stories we hear as children, even if we do not consciously remember them. Our ancestors' voices resonate in our bones.

It is a truism that when we read letters or memoirs written by an ancestor, we discover pieces of ourselves. We may have blue eyes like Great-grandfather and Grandmother's green thumb. Each piece we put in place is a precious part of the gigantic puzzle that is us. Working on our personal puzzle is a daunting task. Much as we try, we can never complete it. We each have over 2,000 direct ancestors in only ten generations. All of them have their own stories to tell. Grandmother Alice shares stories of some of her eight great grandparents — a treasure trove her descendents are fortunate to have.

Those of us who are not her descendents can read books like this one to partially fill empty spaces in our puzzles. Grandmother Alice grew up in South Carolina, but we all had ancestors living in the years about which she wrote. In her voice, we hear echoes. Our ancestors may have lived in the South, in New England or the Midwest. They may have been city dwellers rather than inhabitants of rural communities. They may have been new immigrants rather than descendents of early settlers. Whoever and wherever they were, it is likely that they cooked over open fireplaces, mourned babies who died in infancy and sons who went to war and never returned, spun and wove their cloth, and faced financial crises more or less successfully.

Even those whose ancestors had not yet come to the United States by the 1930s can discover in this book something about the origins of values, attitudes, and customs of the communities where they now live. Grandmother Alice, in telling her own story, touches us as well. The legacy she left is rich. She had a wonderful eye (and ear) for detail and a way with words. She must have loved people and their stories. She describes her ancestors and other residents of Greenville County with humor and good will. I visualize her as a child sitting by lamplight, listening to her parents and grandparents. Her grandson Reese listened as well. Perhaps he inherited his great respect for history and tradition and stories from her. I have heard him spin tales, and I know he has an eye and ear for detail and a way with words. He tells his tales with humor and good will.

He, too, is leaving us a legacy. It may be that the special friendship between Reese Hawkins and Louis L'Amour, about which Mr. Hawkins wrote in *Remembering Louis L'Amour*, blossomed because of traits he inherited from Grandmother Alice. I think she would have taken the L'Amour children, as the Hawkins' did, and shown them the places where their ancestors lived and told them stories of their heritage. I think she would have explored the South Carolina Revolutionary War battlefields and the hills of Tennessee with the L'Amours, as the Hawkins' did. I can imagine L'Amour sitting with her as he listened. Some of her stories might have become episodes or plot lines for his short stories or books. He might have described, for example, a church service where the congregation included the picturesque people of her church. And the preacher in his story might have contrived to let a little boy eat all the chicken he wanted! Grandmother Alice attended school for only twelve months, but her memories enrich us all.

Dr. Linda Lucas Walling
Professor, School of Library and Information Science
University of South Carolina
Columbia, South Carolina

A FRIENDLY WORD TO THE READER

Moving from the wide spacious hall I turned left and walked through the door into the room. The wooden floor was the same as it was 70 years ago. To my left was the same open fireplace where, as a six year old, I warmed myself on a cold winter morning. Red coals from the same fire later in the day cooked a mess of turnip greens in a cast iron pot. The fireplace was now free of ashes and only black scars remained on the bricks.

> [a _mess_ of turnip greens . . . this means a
> quanity of food sufficient for a meal. mess hall is a
> location where a group regularly have meals together.]

This was the room where my grandmother, Alice Crain Hawkins, spent the last years of her life. Frail in body, strong in spirit, she wrote her journal. I looked around the room, stepped over where the head of her bed used to be and turned around. Opposite me was a window that unlocked for her the four seasons of beauty. To the left of that window there used to be a door. This was the one I used to go out into the side yard to play. Now in its place is a bare wall. I looked through the dusty window. The small trees near where I played are now giant oaks. What was once a large vegetable garden is obscured by honey suckle vines clinging to broken down remnants of an old fence.

On my visits to this house during my late teens I would move an old straight back kitchen chair over to the side of her bed. My grandmother would put aside a book she was reading or the memoirs she was writing and tell me stories of her childhood and some she remembered that her grandmother told her. I would listen, and as the years passed I forgot most of them. Many of the stories she told me are the same as she wrote in her memoirs.

These true stories written in the late 1920's and early 1930's give us a fresh, novel and unique understanding of the lives of those who lived in the upper part of South Carolina during the state's growing years. Few ever had such a memory as my grandmother possessed. Her stories published for the first time were written while an invalid during the last years of her life. Her education was limited to the brief common schools of the 1870's and 1880's. Grammar was almost unknown in rural communities at that time and I have not changed her unique style of writing.

In our first book, *Remembering Louis L'Amour,* coauthored by my daughter, Meredith Hawkins Wallin, we used actual conversations taken from audio tapes I made during some of the many times my wife, Margaret, and I were with Louis L'Amour and his family.

In this book, *Grandmother Alice,* I use her memoirs written about the people who settled in the upper part of South Carolina where I was born and spent my youth. During my work on these historical events about which Grandmother wrote, I became a silent grandson once again sitting in the old cane chair by the side of her bed listening as she told her stories. At intervals I have inserted additional stories of my own and also notes of explanation.

Grandmother wrote these stories for two of her sons. Vernon was the older, a graduate of Richmond College. He lived in Greer, South Carolina, was employed by the Federal Land Bank and prior to his retirement was Senior Appraiser supervising those who worked in North Carolina, South Carolina and Georgia. Marcelle, his daughter, now lives in Clemson, South Carolina.

Ansel was the fourth of grandmother's twelve children. After service in the first World War, he earned a law degree at the University of South Carolina and practiced law in Greer with his brother Harper. He served in the state legislature for eleven years and was secretary of the Greenville County delegation.

Hovering in the background of my grandmother's writing was my grandfather, John Landrum Hawkins. I can hear him now as he stood at the foot of the stairs. This wakeup call may have been repeated once as he stood there but never more.

"Connie! Azalee! Cody! Time to get up! There's work to be done!" I was six years old and had slept the night on a pallet on the floor of my Uncle Cody's second floor bedroom. As I was pulling up my pants I heard the back screen door slam. I knew Grandpa had left for the barn. There were two cows to be milked. Before leaving he had started a fire in the kitchen range. The day before I had brought wood in from the woodshed.

When he returned with the pails of milk my aunts had breakfast ready. Fresh homemade biscuits, country sausage, gravy, grits, and sweet milk were ready to be placed on the large kitchen table. (I identify the kind of milk as *sweet* to distinguish it from buttermilk. Lots of buttermilk was consumed in the South). After breakfast four tenant farmers joined Uncle Cody in the back yard near the well floor and I listened as Granddad told each what he wanted them to do. Uncle Cody was to clean the stables. This was my day to be with him.

Cody filled the wagon using a pitchfork, tossing the manure from the stable into the wagon. I sat on the wagon seat and watched. After the wagon was loaded and driven to the field, the manure spreader was engaged and I saw the manure as it was scattered from the rear of the wagon onto the field. There were six stables in the barn, four for horses and mules and two for cows.

This was an all day job and I sat on the wagon seat from beginning to the end. The sun was low in the sky when the team was unhitched and led to the water trough. Upon returning to the house, Granddad took me into the spacious front hall and went to the corner where he kept a small floor safe. He opened it, removed a dollar bill from a compartment and as he handed it to me he said,

"Reese, you have worked hard all day and I want to pay you."

I took the first dollar I ever earned and stuffed it in one of the pockets of my pants. Granddad was a good farmer. He made good use of the information he received from Clemson Agricultural College. He entered state contests and won first place in both cotton and wheat production. He sold some of the wheat he grew to neighborhood farmers for seed.

It was all fun on my visits to my Granddad's farm. I watched as hogs were butchered and observed my Granddad as he worked processing the meat in one of the ten support buildings. This was a one room log structure with space between the logs for air conditioning. Slaughtering was done in the late fall. The inside was protected from rain by a corrugated tin roof.

My uncle Cody killed each hog with a bullet from his 22 rifle. They were lifted off the ground by block and tackle...were dressed out and taken to the curing house.

[dress: to cut up, trim and remove the skin, feathers, viscera, etc., (from an animal, meat, fowl, or flesh of a fowl) for market or for cooking (often followed by 'out' when referring to a large animal]

Granddad prepared his special formula which he rubbed into the meat in the preserving process. When he finished large wooden bins were filled with pork for chops and ribs, breakfast bacon and fatback.

[fatback: chiefly South, Midland, and Southern U.S. the fat and fat meat from the upper part of a side of pork, usually cured by salt.]

Lard was rendered from the fat of the hogs, especially the internal fat of the abdomen. Hanging from the rafters in cloth bags were shoulders and hams. A generous portion of this over the year found its way to our house in Greer and helped feed our family of six.

The pigs bladder was cleaned, dried and served as a pouch for my Granddad's chewing tobacco. In food markets one can still purchase jars of pigs feet.

There were support buildings on the farm . . . the largest was the barn. I explored this from the harness room to the loft. Then there was a building with four stables in the feed lot, at harvest time corn was stored in the corncrib, where it was later shucked on rainy days. A hand driven shelling machine was used to separate the kernel from the cob. The corn was then mixed with wheat and my Grandmother scattered it on the nearby ground for her chickens.

The cotton house was a one room building where the cotton was weighed-in and a record kept of the amount picked by each worker. There was the pump house where water pump and storage tank were kept. Wood was stored here. A piglot or pigpen was where the pigs grew up. One of my cousins told me Granddad would periodically wash the hogs.

He had a place for everything and everything had to be in it's place with one exception . . . the center space in the carriage house. This was where women held their quilting bees. Carriage and buggy were kept in separate storage areas on each side.

How fascinating it was to see him start the fire in the blacksmith shop, hear the bellow and stand on my tiptoes to see the hot particles pop up from the red hot coals. I was permitted to handle and turn the blower.

As I work on my Grandmother's story and recall my own experiences with my relatives, I am certain no modern kindergarten would have taught me what I learned during the times I spent there with the Hawkins Family.

R. H.
Jamestown, ND

1904 - Back: Ansel, John, Vernon, Allan and Alice. Front: John L. Jr., Ernestine, Helen and Harper. Haskell, Cody, Azalee, and Connie were yet to come.

Left: Winter scene in 1918 of new house built in 1906.

Bottom: Grandmother Alice's bedroom behind bush at left.

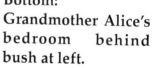

TABLE OF CONTENTS

Chapter 1

This Day October 22, 1931

I have been listening over the radio to Sousa's Band in a concert honoring the memory of Thomas Alva Edison who was buried yesterday. They played a funeral march composed by Beethoven and supposed to be written for Napoleon Bonaparte, Edison's favorite. Edison was very deaf and was heard to say that if he could only hear that would be what he would want played first. Blessings on his memory.

I have lived in a great age, Marcelle. When I was a little girl there were no telephones, no good roads. The main street in Greenville City was almost hub deep in red mud in the winter time. All the county roads were narrow, full of holes, rocks, ruts, and sometimes low stumps.

There were no automobiles, no electric lights, no talking machines, no flying machines, very few sewing machines and very few cook stoves. When I was a little girl I expect the stove and sewing machines could have been counted on the fingers of one

John and Alice

hand here in Highland township. The incomparable Thomas Edison invented over thirteen hundred different things most of them in daily use. Radio had never been dreamed of let alone invented. Now I have grown old and a shut-in — I'm keeping in touch with the whole worlds current events, music, sermons, market reports.

I have heard men in Europe, talking in Europe as plain as if they were in the same room as I. The question is what next? If it were possible for me to live another fifty years, I would love to live that long providing my family could too just to see what would happen next.

I was born on a Thursday February 23, 1871 of poor but respectable parents, the second child a son before me died an infant. If I could have had a hand in selecting a time to be born and live I don't think in the last many great Centuries there has been so many changes as I've seen during my 60 years.

Your dad and I were married the 23 of December 1888 by Rev. R. Wilden. I was in my seventeenth year and he past his eighteenth year. We had grown up together you might say.

When a child there were great bodies of original forests just as the Indians left them except when invaded by cattle or hogs or opossum hunters. Great chestnuts oak and pine skeletons lying molding away, had lain perhaps a century. Sometimes young trees growing up through them feeding on the mold.

Chestnut wood was as lasting as iron in some of the old rail fences . . . those are rails of chestnut which were split a century ago. My Dad said up until a hurricane which descended on this country in August 1845 blowing lots of the oldest Chestnuts down. The Chestnut trees began to die out. Our fields all fenced which was small patches compared to some scary trees "tales" everywhere.

Life was very simply lived. We raised everything on the farm we used except sugar, coffee, etc.

Great Grandfather Crain's House

When I first remember we lived in this big oak log house built of great big oak logs hewed and fitted smoothly daubed with white clay It must have stood the storms of around a century. There were windows with wooden shutters, wide fireplace, stone hearth a roomy upstairs with a shed room on the east side. A kitchen called an ell, a gallery between where our dining table was and in hot weather, a wide fireplace in the kitchen where cooking was done (a separate building joined by a covered walkway).

Also out of this house went four of his grandsons to the Confederate Army. Three to never return. One was a bridge builder (John). He didn't do active fighting but died of disease, malaria or typhoid fever, one, I have understood. So two large families were born and reared within its walls all gone except in memory.

The Earthquake of 1886

August had been a very rainy season but August 31 morning dawned hot, very hot and clear with nothing to indicate what was pending. I will relate my own experiences.

Grandmother was 15 years old at this time.

We went about out daily duties. My Father went to his Uncle Sam Crain's who as it proved his death bed. So Ma was left alone with us children and went to bed as usual and to sleep as usual, only to be awakened by the bedstead rocking. Trembling groaning of the house scraping, squeaking, cracking etc. We didnt know what in the world. It woke the young children who were crying and scared and Ma told them maybe it was a big old hog rubbing its back on the sills of the house.

That pacified the little ones but I knew better. I knew a hog couldn't bring a dead heavy rumbling roaring sound out of the Southeast which encompassed the whole elements and came up in a wave passing over in a way never to be forgotten.

My Ma knew perfectly well what it was. She and I got up and dressed. In a little while Uncle Shade and Aunt Pollyann and their children all came in on their way to the cemetery to be there when the dead arose. That's what Aunty meant to do. Uncle Shade induced her to step up to our house first. She came in with the exclamation.

"Oh Sis (meaning Ma) its the end of time and I am on my way to Hermans grave I want to be there when he raises". Herman being a 20 year old son who had died 4 or 5 years before. My Ma replied, "Why Pollyann its only an earthquake". Uncle Shade said,

"That is what I told her all the time but I couldn't do a thing with her".

That is the first time Ma had told what she knew all the time. She kept perfectly calm, Aunt Pollyann all the time keeping up her weeping and wringing her hands but didn't go to the cemetery.

Pa's experience was (it being a very hot sultry night) the men taking turns sitting by the sick bed. He and some other neighbor men were standing outside. He said all at once their knees began to sway, wobble back and forth. He thought he was having an attack of some kind and wouldn't say anything about it unless it grew worse. My dad didn't like to complain. About that time a man spoke out, "Fellows there is something the matter with my laigs." Another and another all admitted they were feeling the same way immediately following the rumbling sound.. The earthquake was around eleven o'clock at night the minor ones in daytime.

Well it was two or three days before the news reached us abut the Charleston disaster. There was a small depression and smaller gully below our home and there was a beautiful spring of clear water bubbling up and running off and this spring ran on until the next summer. The next day there was a hazy atmosphere, something like Indian summer. This was followed by several quakes up until October.

My sister Lula, a very young girl, told me not long since that she was up at Grandma Mitchell's after the big quake when all at once doors, windows, dishes began rattling. Of course the house was shaking too. She said Grandma told her not to get scared it was only an earthquake. Poor child I suppose she was reconciled. Grandma and Ma too could stay outwardly calm, didn't seem to be the least disturbed when others lost their heads. The folks who were traveling in wagons and buggies didn't know what happened, they heard the roar but didnt know. Some old timers called it 'aithquick'

Well after the earth had reminded you of a sitting hen, all flustered, well when her feathers settled back in place as it were, there was an abrupt change in temperature and a cold wind came out of the Southeast in the same direction the rumbling roaring noise came. Well, I dont know until this day whether it was from excitement or whether it was the sudden drop in temperature but my teeth chattered and I shook in a very embarrassing manner. Ma consoled me with, "Why you only have a chill."

There was also an earthquake in this country in 1812. Severe in Tenn., KY, and past the Mississippi River. For sixty years now there wasn't one so far as I know and I remember 57 years of this time.

Grandmother Alice Introduces Us to Vernon

To Marcelle when your dad was a small boy. Can you imagine a delicate little boy with hair almost as white as cotton, eyes as blue as blue, skin as white as milk which refused to tan even if he did play doctor in the sand pile in the sun wrapping innumerable packages of medicine and bottles of tonic when

**Marcelle Kelly and
daugher, Lauren**

he wasn't driving that invisible four horse team he owned. I was never able to see any of it except the whip which he owned. A cotton string tied to the stick.

He was the best kindest little fellow living in his land of make believe. He was slow about talking, didn't talk any until more than two years old. We had an opossum in a box fattening. He enjoyed watching feed put into the possums prison. He must have been an investigator himself. One day he ran in literally dancing to the tune of <u>posse go oods</u> (possum gone to the woods). I went with him to the scene of the escape and he pointed out a cotton row and its tracks.

Well would you believe it his tongue was loosened. He almost talked me to death afterwards and he has been talking ever since. He wasn't diseased or anything he was small or I mean slender like Margaret Hawkins or Lois Donnan.

An Opossum or Possum is a prehensile-tailed marsupial of the eastern U.S., the female having an abdominal pouch in which its young are carried: noted for the habit of feigning death when in danger.

Oh! If time would only turn backward in its flight and let me enjoy my little blue eyed precious boy only one day. So it's my time to live in a land of make believe that he and the other children are with me and that they are not really nearly all gone when I need their presence most in my feeble shut-in days. Marcelle, I am writing all this lying in bed so please excuse blots of ink and mistakes.

Now We Meet Ansel

This is written for my beloved son, Ansel M. Hawkins. You came into our home at an opportune time. Preston had died in August before you were born in April. You (as far as one baby can take another's place) were in the cradle and your presence was a benediction to us as you spent your time eating and sleeping.

So one day I carried you to a Mitchell Reunion between the ages of 3 or 4 months. You walled your frightened gray eyes around and cried and cried and cried causing me to be very uneasy but upon reaching home you showed all indications that you wanted to nestle down, after cooing and gurgling, for a prolonged sleep.

My next most distant memory was about you after you could speed over the floor in your heelless shoes with your flaxen hair which had a scalp lock that waved like a plume. (Boys of your size wore long hair then). And how you hollered in the late afternoon to be carried outside which you dearly loved..

And after you learned to talk you asked questions that agnostics, scientists divines have never been able to answer let alone an ignoramus like me. "Who made God?" etc. You liked preachers as you went to church from the time you were large enough to go but where you refused to stay until attention was attracted to the antics of the preacher such as pounding the book board etc.

Rev. R. B. Vaughn was one of whom you admired when you were about two and a half or three years old. I bathed you and put on your gown one night, and looking over your shoulder at your sweeping gown you said, "Now I guess I look like Vaughn". (You called him Vaughn.) And that was the first we knew you admired the long preachers coat.

One Saturday meeting Vaughn was invited home for dinner. We were only going to have one chicken for dinner. Of course we had other things too but you were inclined to act

Vernon, Ansel and Allan - 1902

piggish by not eating anything but chicken so I had given you a certain lecture before you went to church with your daddy. It so happened you rode home with Vaughn so you told him I said for you to ask for only one piece of chicken and you wanted him to see you got more.

So when dinner was announced Mr. Vaughn says, "I want Ansel to eat by me today". So your high chair was placed beside him instead of being at my side. So Mr. Vaughn passed and repassed the chicken to you asking in his holiest manner if you wouldn't have more so you scandalized us by eating five or six pieces.

Another preacher came home with your dad for dinner (his name escapes me). You rode with him and when he entered the door he was laughing and said "I hear we are to have ginnea for dinner." I asked him how he knew and he nodded at you.

Your dad petted you so if he went to church he would take you that is if you wanted to go whether I wanted to or not.

You gave a long recitation at a school entertainment

when you were near 5 years old. You were secretary of the Sunday School when still in knee pants. You never seemed to suffer from self consciousness. There were several years you were my right hand man helping with the cattle and hogs etc. Allan and Vern being off in school. All the drudgery fell on my and your lot.

You were always, after you grew old enough, obedient and kind to me. I felt so over worked and nervous at times or was it just plain cussedness? I am afraid I scolded you when you didn't deserve it and if I ever hurt your feelings I humbly beg your pardon for you were a beloved son (and you are yet in this year 1929).

Ansel's two black books -
Purchased at Calhoun Office Supply, Spartanburg, SC.

Chapter 2

Great Grandfather
William Crain's Peculiarities
He came from England —
entitled to Coat of Arms.

Motto, *"How So Ever God Pleases."*

He counted himself as being a staunch Baptist went to church etc. until the church elected a preacher and voted to pay him a salary. He declared he wouldn't listen to any man preach who would accept filthy lucre so he stayed away from church ten years. He was very careful to read his Bible. He must have left England on account of religious persecution. He had a spite who smacked at anything like a Catholic Priest who lived off the people. The funny part of it was, he accumulated lots of filthy lucre besides having all the land for miles around.

He was six feet high hard fisted and outspoken. He had fair skin and blue eyes. I suppose red headed as many of his descendants had red hair. His hair was snow white when he grew old.

He was a soldier in the Revolutionary War. I failed to question grandmother about it so its traditional. In talking one day she said that her father fought in the Revolution and her husband escaped and then her sons fought in the Confederacy. Only being a child and not interested I failed to ask if he was at Kings Mountain, Cowpens, etc.

Great Grandfather William came from Suffolk, England

in 1758 to Charleston, South Carolina. He removed from Charleston near where Johnie Crain now lives sometime any where from 1760 and 1770 exact date not known.

He established good relationships with the Indians. They were still here up to the time his son Samuel was bitten supposedly by a mad dog. His Indian neighbors treated him for the bite by immersing him in a hogshead up to his neck in brine for nine days. I don't know for how long at a time. Anyway the treatment was effective because he lived to be ninety odd years, ninety three I think.

> *A hogshead is a container shaped like a large barrel*
> *especially like one containing from 63 to 140 gallons of liquid.*

He must have had some pride about his girls personal appearance as he imported silks and satins from England for his red headed, brown eyed daughters. I think three out of the four had red hair and brown eyes. One of his sayings was, "a brown or black eyed person couldn't see as well as a blue eyed one". This may have been to tease his wife.

He dressed in George Washington style, knee britches, leggings etc. He lived on after that period but like lots of old fellows kept the old style.

He must have been the spokesman for the family, didn't hear of Great Grandmother expressing herself in anyway. He out lived her some years, don't know how many. He was very old when he died. I knew him as Grand Pap Crain. That is what my dad called him.

He eventually built a cabin near John Crains home, later moving near where Woodfin Barton now lives in a large substantial house which I remember very well.

He married Miss Mary Farmer, don't know whether he brought his wife from England, married her in Charleston or whether she was already here but I doubt her being here. She had coal black hair and dark eyes, either brown or black. Don't know whether he secured a land grant or not. He bought land at 12 1/2 cents an acre. Yes twelve and a half cents per acre and he gave each child (I think he did) as he gave great-Grandfather he must have owned about 2500 acres. He had two grandchildren who resided in his home and they shared equally with his children who were:

William - who was a Baptist Preacher.
Shadrack - called Shade, who was also a Baptist Preacher. He was the Grandfather of Shade, Dean, and Buford Crain.
Samuel - died in 1886 in his 92 or 93 year.
Dennis - my paternal Grandfather who died in 1857, age 66 years.
Charles - walked out the door one day and never seen again. His father willed him part of his estate. I do not know if he left before his parents died or slipped away from his brothers and sisters after the death of his parents.
Judy - married a Dill.
Rebecca - "Becky" married Jay Mitchell and moved west.
Molly - married a Dill.
Huldah - married a Watson.

William Crain raised tobacco, I think that was his money crop. There was a way of packing tobacco in hogsheads and that had some kind of two wheeled trucks or rollers they called them I think. He carried this to Charleston. He grew corn and wheat.

When he first came to America he reaped his grain with a scythe and had what was known as a threshing floor. There was not such a thing as a threshing machine so this dry grain was scattered around in a circle and oxen and horses were driven around and around until the grain was tramped out. The next process was select a windy day. The grain was thrown up and allowed to fall on cloth on the ground. Up and down, up and down until the chaff all blew away, all blew away.

Mosteller Mill

The story of grain harvesting as it was done in Old Testament times may be found in the first chapter of the book of Ruth. Winnowing was one step in this process my grandmother's ancestors used here in the early settlement of our country.

I didn't hear but I expect they threshed for others as it required a substantial tight floor that didn't leak. I might say while on the subject that Mosteller Mill is among one of the oldest if not the oldest in the country.

February of 1960 found me boarding a plane in North Dakota where we lived and in a few hours I arrived in the foothills of the Blue Ridge Mountains. This section of South Carolina was well in the midst of a profound change. No longer were cotton farmers in the fields working their way along the rows of plants, chopping the encroaching weeds and grass. Many farmers and their descendants were working in manu-facturing plants.
The migration of industry started after World War II and

by the early sixties the shadows of these industrial plants spread out all over Greenville County. My dad, Allan Hawkins, who was the oldest child of Grandmother Alice, lived just a short distance from Mosteller Mill. He would often visit there. One day during my visit I joined him for the short trip to see this old building alongside a river. A single gas pump stood 20 feet from the front entrance. The glass tank that held the gas was filled by pushing a long upright handle horizontally back and forth. Once the level of the gas reached the top mark one could, through an attached hose, begin putting gas into the tank of a car.

We entered the building. I noted a few can goods on three or four shelves just inside the door. Next to them tobacco and snuff. Pausing I noted the brand names on the chewing tobacco and snuff . . . Tube Rose, Peach, Bloodhound, Apple, Sweet Society, Railroad Mills, Navy . Then there were a few cans of pork and beans, salmon, black-eyed peas, Vienna sausage, soda crackers and bags of grits.

Ahead of us was the old machinery that still ground the corn, and to the right was an old pot-bellied stove. Gathered around the stove in addition to Mr. Mosteller, the mill owner and operator, were several of the old timers I remembered from my youth. Greetings were exchanged and I took their offer of the best seat available, an ancient straight chair, worn smooth from its many years of use.

I looked around and in one corner was a large pile of corn cobs that served as fuel for the pot bellied stove. Another corner was filled with corn . . . near that a shelling machine. Glancing up I noted a big cat, content, dozing in the warmth of the upper layer of air that surrounded his position on one of the rough beams.

Shortly after we arrived my dad spoke to the owner. "Brother Mosteller, I need some gas in the car, reckon you can fill it up." Brother Mosteller's expression did not change. He gave no indication he had heard the request. We talked for some ten minutes about the state of the weather, what winter in North Dakota was like, what kind of flight I had, and they asked me questions about my family. During a pause, Dad said, "I think it will take a quart of oil."

Mr. Mosteller, without any reaction to a customer's request for service, continued to ask questions about a section of the country that was some 1600 miles from the area he knew. Another five or ten minutes passed before he

This snuff was bought at Mosteller Mill.

slowly got up and said to Dad, "I'll go out and put some gas in your car, Allan."

Within eight or nine miles of Interstate 85 and a large regional airport there still existed an old water fed wheel that furnished power for a corn mill and an atmosphere of relaxation and contentment for those who gathered there.

How Great Grandfather Crain's Money Was Divided After His Death

Marion Neeves Hawkins, Mrs. Ansel Hawkins, examined some old time land titles and wills. She found William Crain's will or copy of it. William Crain died in 1841. His estate was settled in 1841, 1842, or 1843.

Grandmother (remember I called her Mother like Pa did. My own mother I called Ma) told me that for small change, a silver dollar Mexican I believe, was cut in half for half dollars, 4 pieces for quarters and 8 pieces for 12 1/2 cents. These were known as pieces of 8. The money must have been reduced to slivers. Great Grandfather had accumulated quite a bit of gold and silver. He was counted as wealthy. His land was not counted for much.

Mother told me she was there the day the money was divided. She said the sons and daughters sat in a circle around a small table with the money on it. Anyway the heirs seated themselves and a disinterested person took the money and measured it with a pint cup shaking and smoothing it as near equal as he could. The women held theirs in their laps the men held theirs in their hats. I failed to hear how many pints there were. The modern hat crown wouldn't have held much but the old bell crown style held much more. Gold was not chipped up.

The reason I remember so well the pint cup was passed around several times. Ma said her stepdaughter Polly who shared with the sons and daughters, anyway Pop had a pair of expressive shoulders so mother said. Every time the pint cup was emptied into Polly's lap she shrugged her shoulder. All this took place anywhere from 1838 to 1840.

Six miles away is North Greenville Academy, now North Greenville College. Home to many of the family through the years.

Scene taken from road in front of college.
Southern tip of Blue Ridge Mountains in background.

Chapter 3

Shadrack Hid His Money

Shadrack Crain was born in 1794. He married Sallie Watson. They reared a large family and accumulated quite a bit of money. In time of the Civil War some raiders went to his house to rob him. He refused to tell where his money was hidden. They told him they would kill him if he didn't tell. He still refused so they kicked, knocked and beat him without results. They procured a rope carried him to a convenient tree tied it around his neck and would pull him up by the neck and then let him down and say, "Now tell". So up to this time, the year of our Lord 1929, he hasn't told. His money, gold and silver was tied up in a bundle of rags or old ragged clothes hanging to the rafters of an outbuilding.

They finally left him half dead so his mind cracked whilst he wasn't a raving lunatic he was never well any more and in 4 or 5 years died. It was supposed to be the brothers from a local family and their gang. When the men began to come back from the army they became uneasy and slipped out of the country. I noticed not long since in reading about Kansas City and its old timers the same brothers were mentioned as doing a big business as cattle shippers so I guess that is where they slipped off to.

Great Uncle Billie Crain

Great Uncle Billie Crain, Shade's brother preached, supplied churches and married couples for years. He said it always frightened him to perform a marriage ceremony, so he held to a chair to steady himself. I remember seeing this paternal great uncle one time. And if it hadn't been forcibly impressed on my mind by a minor accident I don't suppose I would have remembered him at all.

It was this way. I a child I venture to say not more than three years about four years old at Grandmother Crain's. Uncle Billie entered the big house off the front and as he came in Mother met him with hand extended and he coming on the other side holding out his hand — well that handshake didn't materialize.

The door was low (as so many of them were in old houses) although he was reared in this one he forgot to duck his head and he being tall gave it an awful bump. And the way Mother assisted him to a chair saying Oh Billie I am so sorry she rubbed his head with camphor and all the time saying Billie I am so sorry are you better? etcs. I all the time staring in wide eyed astonishment not knowing who Billie was and seeing mother's kindness.

I can see him so plain as if it was yesterday. He was tall with snow white hair benevolent clean shaven round face (with a rosy completion or that may have been the result of the bump) with the prettiest pansy blue eyes. He was dressed in a black Prince Albert suit I suppose that is the name of the style anyway frock coat and he wore a tall beaver or maybe silk hat like our Presidents in inaugural parades. All old timers who dressed in style wore them but I never saw many of them.

Don't think Uncle Billie lived long enough after that it was the only time I ever remember seeing him but I remember two incidents at his funeral (he was buried at the Crain burying ground beside his wife and six children). His casket was carried by the pall bearers from either Mother's old home or the road and I and a little cousin joined hands and walked skipped and ran right in front of the coffin. I must have got a scolding or I wouldn't have remembered it.

Another thing was one of his daughters was standing by a tree weeping, her face covered and her shoulders shaking. I went in front of her and peeked and peeked trying to see how her face looked doing it as she kept her face covered with handkerchief, veil etc. I know now that she was weeping. I don't think I knew then. After I did this I felt I had done the wrong thing.

Uncle must have been nearly ninety when he died. He married Sallie Sparks. Mother always spoke of her as Sister Sallie as she was her half sister and think quite a bit younger than Uncle Billie but she preceded him a good many years he married again and left a wife and two daughters.

Mother said her sister was a beautiful woman of her type she had jet black wavy hair fair complexion and blue eyes tall and slender. Being her only living sister she was very devoted to her and talked about her as long as she lived they marrying brothers the tie between the two families was very close.

Will close with a fright Uncle Billie got once. His home was west or is it south of Mayes Bridge. Anyway he owned land on is it South Tiger river and as I say his home site isn't far from the bridge. (Let me say here Pa said when he was a boy this river had lots of fishing holes and lots of fish).

Anyway over in the Sandy Flat vicinity near the big road was a so called haunted spot. It was in woods and once upon a time a man had committed suicide by hanging himself on a tree near this road.

My uncle was not at all superstitious so the story goes when the folk told him about it he poo hooed the idea. The thing had chased a neighbor by the name of Abe Collins.

One dark night uncle Billie was riding horseback alone returning home he said when he was passing the place he attached so little importance to the tales told he had his mind elsewhere. When all at once there was a thud on the ground as the slamming of a log. His horse was badly frightened gave a leap as something jumped up behind him and calmly sitting on the horses hips was a apparition like moon shine shaped like a dog, its eyes glittered yellowly at him he hollered struck at it with his riding whip etc. but failed to dislodge it. It stayed with him all the way (I imagine matched Ichabod Crane) in his wild ride.

When he couldn't get rid of it and his horse almost frightened to death he became frightened almost to death too. Anyway this horse ran three or four miles and when reaching home instead of going to the gate that led to the lot and stables it jumped a ten rail fence. The family hearing the commotion ran out and had to help him off the horse. He was so scared he was speechless. Every time he looked back into those glittering eyes it got worse and worse but after he reached home there was nothing visible but a badly frightened man and winded horse. I would make a guess it was a nesting hooting owl. He and Uncle Sam was the only ones I remember seeing.

Great Uncle Sam outlived him by several years. I remember seeing him several times. Went with one of my aunts to spend the day with him and his wife Aunt Lottie Ann and a widowed and an old maid daughter. We had a day I never forgot. The old fashioned house old furniture dishes etcs. He was then ninety years old and his little roly poly apple checked wife was very old too but not as old as he. Uncle Sam looked over six feet tall with white grey hair large brown or black eyes. I and he talked nearly all day. He seemed to fall in love with me and gave me a nice present afterward.

He was an outspoken gruff hard fisted man and had accumulated quite a bit of money in real estate mortgages and land. He was a church member but from tradition he wasn't an easy mark but looked well after No. 1. They had a rather large family but had several sons killed in the civil war. He died in 1886, 93 years old I think or maybe 94. He is buried at

Camp Creek Church there is an error of dates on the tombstone either date of birth or death unless the family had it corrected.

Dennis Crain

My grandfather their brother was Dennis Crain. I calculate he was born about 1791. He married a Miss Mary Crain a cousin of his (distant one so said). There were two children, girl and a boy. The mother was a red headed woman she and the little boy died and was buried on the John Forrester place the graves are obliterated. He was left with a little redheaded girl, Polly, (Pop) for short.

She was reared by Great Grandfather and he willed her an interest in his estate equal with his own children. Great Grandmother died years before him and his children married off. I've an idea his two Grand Children Pop and John Watson stayed with Great Grandfather as he died in his own home didn't break up housekeeping.

Fence Grandmother Alice stands by kept the small children off Ridge Road.

Chapter 4

We Come to My Beloved Mother of Blessed Memory Lydia Ann Cothran Crain

My beloved paternal Grandmother Lydia Ann Cothran Crain was born the 13th of June 1804. She married Dennis Crain when she was a mere girl after his first wife died. She was the mother of thirteen children, seven daughters and six sons: Jasper Newton, John, Shadrack (Shade for short), William Daniel (My father), Enos M, Henderson Good, Cynthana called Cynthia, Clementina, Narcissi, Judy, Angeline, Elizabeth, and Martha.

She told me about her own maternal Grandfather or the truth is I gathered these facts from her talk. I could have gathered a lot more if I had been interested. Anyway she would in talking tell about visiting Granddad Cooley. She said he was a full blooded Spaniard was dark skinned with a blue cast or tinge or what ever you call it.

She said her Grandmother was a fat redheaded Irish woman but silly like I forgot to ask her what her maiden name was. She said they were wealthy, lived in a brick house and owned lots of slaves as it was known. I don't know how many children there were. Only heard two mentioned, her Mother Judy and Aunt Betsy.

Lydia Ann was a typical pioneer. She was tall, had a beautiful complexion, hair that grew thin but refused to turn grey. She had the prettiest blue eyes and the kindest, sweetest expression in the world. She was one of the most industrious persons I ever knew, working from morning until retiring at night. Grandfather had a clause in his will that should she need anything she could sell some land.

The Civil War left her bereft of three sons. She owned a corn mill but with all the menfolk gone for four years the machinery went down and wouldn't run anymore. The raiders (a band of bad men who went through the country stealing) took her last horses. You know, I never heard her mention selling land. She managed to get her patches plowed, of corn, cotton and potatoes. She hoed, pulled fodder, picked cotton and in between she raised sheep, hogs and some cattle.

> *As a small boy I sat in the shade of oak tree on the edge of a field of corn. Earlier when I asked Uncle Doc what Granddad meant when he said they were going to — 'pull fodder', he said, "Just climb in the wagon and go with us." I watched as Doc and each of his helpers started down separate rows of corn. He would reach up to the top of the plant and with one hand on each side strip downward collecting the corn leaves in the process. When they had as much as each hand would hold they put the leaves together and slipping two or three of the leaves up, would tie all in a bundle. Then the upper part of the stalk would be snapped down and the bundle would be forced down on the bent stalk. At a later time these bundles were hauled to the barn and fed to the cows.*

She carded, spun and wove bed spreads, blankets, window curtains and woolen cloth for their winter dresses. She also made cotton cloth for their summer wear. She raised a patch of indigo each year to dye the cloth with. She knitted stockings, both wool and cotton, shawls and gloves. At the age of eighty she would pick up an axe, cut down a pole of wood, shoulder it and carry it home to cut into stick lengths. I never heard her say she had a hard time in my life.

She would work hard all week and weather permitting would go to church on Sunday. If the weather was bad she would read her Bible all morning. Sometimes reading it aloud to me. She read it this way. Take the word neither, she would say "nither", the word either she would say "Ither", the word looked was pronounced as a word of two syllables—Look-ed etc. Child-like I remember her pronunciation better than the scripture she read.

I was her special pet. As it happened she loved me more than any of her Grandchildren. I was allowed the privilege of spending one night in the week with her. I loved her almost better than I did my own mother she had entered her second childhood. Her mind was running back so I owe most all that I have written here to her. She enjoyed talking old times and she had a ready listener in me.

Lydia Ann's Family

Lydia Ann had two brothers, John and David Cothran, who moved west. Her maternal Grandfather was Jacob Cooley. Jacob Cooley lived in a brick house and owned a Negro quarter. His children called themselves The Blue Hen's Chickens because their father had a bluish cast or complexion. Jacob Cooley and his red headed wife were my Great, Great Grandparents. Their home was either in lower Greenville or upper Laurens County.

> One of Grandmother Alice's daughters, Helen Forrester, in her research found Jacob willed a Spanish doubloon to each of his Grandchildren.

Mother's mother, Judy Cooley Cothran owned slaves. One Negro woman Dorcas was the cook there were other Negro women as well as men. The others worked in the fields as well as spin and weave. Mother said at night these woman would be running three or four spinning wheels at a time. Some would be carding. I do not suppose you remember how the spinning wheel whirred. She said her stepfather Daddy Sparks would go to the kitchen removed from the other part of the house to keep from hearing them. I might add that I never knew a man who would not walk out when a wheel started. The dust and the lint made one's nose itch besides the noise.

Great Grandmother was a mid-wife. Mother said she had a specially constructed cart and drove a big old gentle horse the cart was called a chair. Overseeing the darkies and going her rounds among the sick was all she did. I will wager she never cooked in her life.

Mother said Dorcas usually woke her mornings chopping sugar off a big cake like cheese cake for their coffee. It was maple sugar.

When the Stars Fell

Mother told me about the excitement in 1833 when the so called STARS FELL. Great Grandmother Cothran was still living at that time she lived below Greenville City. There were several Negro quarters in hearing of them. She was awakened suddenly by groans shouts and prayers. Her own Negroes and others all over the settlement thought it was judgment day or night so the case might be. She said the whole element was filled with what looked like stars shooting and falling. She went out and watched for a while. She also thought it was the judgment so she returned to bed. She said this scripture come into her mind. Revelations the 22nd chapter the eleventh verse.

"He that is just let him be just still. He that is filthy let him be filthy still and he that is righteous let him be righteous still. He that is Holy let him be Holy still".

She thought her doom was sealed that it was too late to pray so she went to bed and dropped off to sleep. She must have died about two years later 1835 or 1836. She was buried near her home somewhere in the lower part of Greenville County.

Another item on the stars. In addition the whole

firmament was full of meteorites. There were fiery red streaks like lightening and sounds like distant cannonading. There was a religious revival in South Carolina and Georgia that was said to have lasted for two years.

One more incident in Great Grandmothers life that I remember. She was on her death bed and they had the windows darkened. She asked the nurse to open the west window so she could see the sun set one more time. No one thought her seriously ill. When the nurse returned from another room she had fallen asleep that knows no waking.

I had forgotten to say she was thrice married. She first married Daniel Cothran. Four of their children died (Cynthia, Cullen, Martha, Jake). She had one daughter by her second marriage, Sallie Sparks, who married Great Uncle Billy Crain. She married another Cothran kinsman of her first husband. They lived at the William Bomar Place (their summer home I suppose). So ends the story of my muchly married Great Grandmother. Peace to her ashes.

Lydia Ann Cothran's Husband Dennis Crain

Grandfather was a tall man with jet black hair and gray eyes and white teeth that were still sound when he died at the age of 66. His hair or I should have said his forehead ran far back in nooks (no lowbrow) you see.

His traits of character were altogether different to his father and brother Sam. Whilst they got along and lived well, if he had been economical he could and would have left more of this world's goods. He was hospitable, helped support the church and preacher if they did accept filthy lucre. Was deacon of church, one of the founders of Pleasant Hill moving his and Mothers membership from Washington Church. (Washington and Tiger churches being the two oldest churches in upper Greenville then).

He prayed in public and exhorted the sinners. He was an easy mark financially. Mother said every one in distress, hungry or wanted him to go on a note just anything he could do he couldn't or wouldn't say no. He went by the name of Uncle Den among neighbors, his nephews and nieces. For instance there was an old neer-do- well in the community came over one day and said,

"Uncle Den, I'm hungry and haint any meet. I want to buy that heifer of yours on a credit. I'll shore pay you jest as soon as I git it."

Mother said they went out to finish their discussion. She said she happened to look out and saw the man driving the beef out of the lot. She said it flew mad over her. She marched out and called the man by name asked him if he saw that lot gate. He admitted he saw it so she ordered him to drive it back and to drive it back then. She told him she knew he didn't aim to pay for it and he knew he didn't pay his honest debts. He drove the yearling back into the lot, pulled off the rope and sneaked off. Well she said afterward she felt she had shown off but didn't regret it. She said they worked and paid their debts and she didn't aim to have Dennis imposed upon.

You would think by this description that Mother was <u>hard</u> boiled and not sympathetic but she used discretion. She didn't have any sympathy for folks who wouldn't work. She was a good nurse and helped the neighbors in sickness and would divide with anyone who was worthy and in need.

Grandfather, according to some old papers I've come across, owned 250 acres of land and a good deal of it cleared and fenced. He operated a corn mill and operated a gold mine and a distillery. He wasn't land hungry as all outdoors was pasture. Cattle hogs and sheep were marked and turned out in the spring. Each man in the neighborhood had different brands and were not rounded up until fall. All down Jordon road around Mt. Lebanon Church, up and down the Mcbee bottoms and goodness knows where all was called the range. In fact all the big outdoors was free the fields being fenced so there really wasn't a necessity for owning a lot of land except for agricultural purposes.

As I said, Grandfather ran a distillery and had six sons and six daughters. He made what was known as a stew Christmas morning. It was a concoction of ginger sugar and whiskey boiled together. They would all gather around the sideboard and he served each one a dram. He considered it a disgrace to get drunk and looked down on drunkenness and strange to say not a single one of those sons made a drunkard.

Also, when the preacher visited him he would give him a drink before returning to the church. And also the ministers were often given a jug of whiskey on their salary. I wonder how that would work now.

Uncle Den died without ever once thinking of intemperance wrong except when a man got drunk. I didn't hear whether Great Grandfather Crain drank or not but suppose he did being so lately from Europe. But I feel sure he was no drunkard. Uncle Sam, Billie and Shade being so far as I know teetotalers. I know one thing. His children loved, reverenced his memory. Father as they all called him as long as he lived and Mother's pet name for him was Dennie. He seemed a living presence to her. In talking it was what Dennie said, how Dennie would like this or that although she outlived him 28 years.

In the spring of 1857 he contracted pneumonia. He had a deathbed scene. Madam Sallie Pennington told me she was there. After calling his family and neighbors around the bed she said she never heard such a prayer. He prayed for his church, his children and for the welfare of the community. After it was over he promptly died. Poor man, if he had only known to have prayed in secret and conserved his strength he might have lived a long time. He was a very healthy strong man up to that time. I have heard he was 66 years old but I believe he was older.

After I was grown up and married I'd heard so much said about Uncle Den I decided to ask an outsider what kind of man he really was. So I asked Granddad Jeffie Mitchell to tell me confidentially what manner of man Dennis Crain was anyway. I shall never forget his reply. (His pet name for me was Allie) so he said, "Allie, he was one of the best men I ever knew." I told him maybe his family after his death had exaggerated notions of his kindness and goodness to them.

He lies beside Grandmother in the old Crain burying ground. Mother's request was to bury her just as close to him as they could so when the men dug her grave it was dug down by the box that held his coffin.

Uncle Enos studied Music and led the singing in the church. He was never married but was engaged to a young lady when he volunteered for the Civil War. He was in the 16th South Carolina regiment as was my Father. He died of hardships and starvation.

Uncle Good was the youngest of the boys. He played the violin. He volunteered and entered the War as a boy in his teens.

Aunt Cynthia was never married. She lived to be 66 years of age. She was a devout Christian. When the young men would come to see her she would talk to them about their souls welfare. She was much more interested in religion than in **getting married.**

Chapter 5

The Civil War
April 1861 — April 1865

Mothers troubles all came at once. She saw four sons enter the Confederate Army. My daddy, Uncle Shade, Enos and Good. Grandfather died in 1857. After a large family of menfolk there were none left, just she and her daughters, a Negro woman and her three boys they had to go to the fields, cut their wood, all kinds of heavy work.

In 1863 I think it was Uncle Enos died of I guess starvation and hardships and is buried at Jackson, Mississippi. My daddy lay a long time with typhoid while in training.

Uncle John was the next oldest. He moved West when a young man or rather he followed the railroads. He was a bridge builder. They were called swinging bridges. He built bridges of the Red River, Tennessee River and Tombigee. These are the tributaries of the Mississippi. He married Miss Ezell and died childless. Sometimes during the war he became sick with I think malaria so he started home through the country going to his mothers. His wife wrote Mother a pitiful letter. After traveling some days he grew suddenly worse and died. So she bought a lot and buried him returning home to her parents. I don't know where he is buried, either eastern Mississippi or western Alabama.

During the war Mother lost her daughter Judy, sons Enos and John. Uncle Good was killed in the last battle on the western battle front, was shot six times. One of his buddies, a Mr. Pittman said he helped carry him off the battle field, said he lived a week. Mr. Pittman said he realized he was mortally wounded and that he didn't mind so much dying if it was not for leaving his mother and sisters. They needed his help so much. He was killed in one of the last battles fought by the Southern Forces and was buried at Jefferson, Tennessee. I think it is called Jefferson City now.

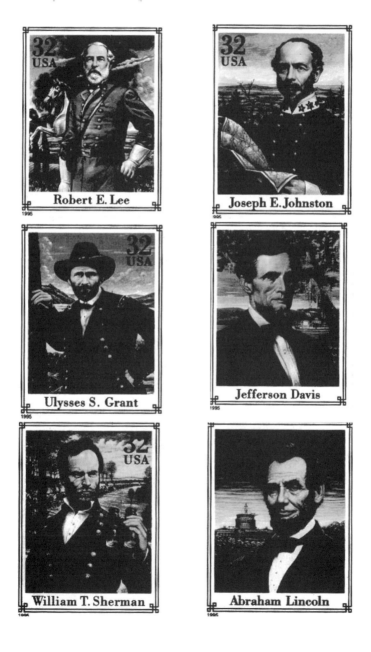

June 12, 1936
Uncle Shade Survives as My Daddy Did

Dear old Uncle Shadrack. My father's brother was called Uncle Shade by us and Shadie by his mother.

He left a young wife and small son to enter the Confederate Army. He chose to go to Virginia or Pennsylvania or both. Pa and his brothers went to the Western front in Georgia and Tennessee.

Uncle Shade was in the battle of Seven Pines and others around Richmond, Virginia. He told us of a time the Confederates were all killed as they marched up a hill side in close formation. He said there was not a man left standing around him. He lay down and pulled dead men up to him and around. He said he could hear bullets hitting those dead men. He was wounded in the head. I suppose in that battle but I have forgotten. He miraculously lived to get home but he looked old and worn from the time I could remember him. I loved him dearly.

He told us when the word came that Lee had surrendered his remnant of comrades were near an apple tree. They went hysterical and tore the apple tree up each taking a piece home in his pocket.

We had a neighbor, a young married man who had left a wife and small child at home. He was in the Cavalry. When the surrender came he was allowed to bring his rack of bones called a horse, home. It was late spring. When he arrived home he found two bushels of Irish potatoes and planted them. He found enough corn to keep himself and wife from starving until the potatoes came in He couldn't find any more corn and they didn't have a bite of bread until the corn grew but the potatoes. There was no horse feed so they grazed the horse.

Most of the fighting was done behind a barricade of logs known as breastworks but when they were whipped out and had to retreat the bullets cut off twig limbs of trees, etc. As my Daddy grew older he would sit at night reminiscing on the war. It would take a large history to hold all he told us of battles that lasted days to what he called skirmishes. He told about when a battle of several days raged of the dead unburied men and horses.

Sometimes conditions would become such there would be called a truce of so many hours so each side could bury its dead, only to resume fighting again. He said a many of a night he would boil a kettle of water pour it to kill cooties, known as body lice, over his shirt, roll up in his blanket with this wet shirt on, lie down on the ground and go to sleep. He told of the forced marches double quicking, of searching around where the horses fed in the hopes of finding a grain of corn to parch. Pa was in the 16th South Carolina Regiment.

We listened as he told of the pangs of thirst, homesickness, cold, and indigestion. When they were in camp on the daily ration of one pint of corn meal a day and a little slice of beef. He said he soon learned his pint of meal went much farther cooked into mush. He said after some of the big battles and after the battle would cease, he could hear groans, cries and pleas for water, water just as far away as their voices would carry. He said in the distance it sounded like frogs in a swamp. He followed this by saying he hated to make that comparison.

The soldiers on both sides would unfold a white flag long enough to carry off the dead and wounded. There were not enough stretcher bearers to carry all off at once so the boys would be running all over the battle field giving water and assisting the wounded and dying.

I asked how in the world he could stand it. He said he became hardened. He said one time after they had the Yankees on the run not giving them time to bury their dead he remembered sitting down to eat his scanty meal, a dead Yankee right near on one side and a dead horse on the other. Seeing a dead man didn't have any more effect on him than a clod of dirt. He said some men broke under the strain and would turn to screaming mad lunatics. It must have been the older men.

The Confederacy finally drafted men from 16 to 60. I think all men under 50 were drafted from the start.

I don't think such a tattered army ever existed as the Confederate Army. Pa said they were a (I mean at the last I think two years) ragged foot sore lousy hungry sick and by that time felt they were fighting a lost cause and were overwhelmingly out numbered in men money and food. But he said when a battle started with their military band playing Dixie with the color bearer carrying the old Confederate flag aloft and all the boys shouting and giving the rebel yell he said he yelled every time he shot. He said the Yankees said they couldn't stand that D-m-d rebel yell. Very often the color bearers would be shot down only to be taken up by some other brave man. He said there were more dead and wounded lying by the flag than any other spot on the battlefield.

I forgot to say he said they were the bravest, kept up their spirits and just full of patriotism and it was battle after battle as there were so many Yankees to whip and so few Confederates to whip them.

He trained at Fort Moultrie, South Carolina and contracted Typhoid. After lying several weeks more dead than alive he was carried home to Mother to recuperate and when the stretcher bearers deposited their burden on the bed Mother didn't know him. Told them she was afraid they had brought someone else. He was so unlike the 174 or 175 pounder who had volunteered a few short months before reduced to a living skeleton but under her and his sisters kind ministration he soon returned to the army but he never saw another well day.

The fever settled in his left leg but that was the reason the Yankees captured him seven months before the war closed. He said they were on a forced march all day and into the night. He said if there had been a gun pointed at his head he couldn't have gone further so he stepped off the side of the road and lay down behind a small pine aiming to join his division as soon as he had rested his lame leg a bit. He had been losing sleep. In fact that was in the night so he accidentally fell asleep.

After he woke with a start at daylight and peeked out into the road that was literally swarming with blue coats. He said he jerked his head but not before a Yankee spied him and shouted, "Hello John Reb, consider yourself under arrest so he was sent to a federal prison in Indianapolis, Indiana to spend eleven months in prison. He didn't get out as soon as war closed. There was a lot of red tape to go over he was released He was so starved and emaciated it was the second time his mother didn't recognize him. The prisoners were starved and mistreated. If a prisoner disobeyed in the least thing he was shot down like a dog. They said they would give them tit for tat for the way their prisoners were treated at another prison at Andersonville.

Sometimes a Southerner would desert and go to the northern side and when they did he was sent back into the north and given his freedom and was called a refugee. My dad did not like men of that type. And he with his buddies had a horror of being taken prisoner. As I have said he was with the 16th South Carolina Regiment. Lets see how many major battles I remember him being in.

> Natchez, Miss. Vicksburg, Miss. (a long seige).
> Kennesaw Mountain.
> Resaca. (Gettysburg, Uncle shade was in this).
> Corinth, Miss.
> From Vicksburg they went to Tenn. where he was in
> the battle of Chickamauga.
> All around Lookout Mountain, Missionary Ridge.

He seemed to have a charmed life. A bullet went through the top knot in his Confederate cap, bullet went through his coat, cut limbs and things off trees around his head besides he said he could hear the bullets whine by like mad bees and he didn't get scratched. Out of his company only twenty men returned home at the close. More men were lost from sickness caused from starvation, typhoid, etc. than from bullets.

Will refer you to History to assort the federal commanders from the Confederate ones. Pa talked of Stuart, Lee, Hood, Rosecrans, Hooker, Bragg, Buell, Johnston, Pickett and Jackson.

General Robert E. Lee visited their division once. They were formed into lines and Lee rode between them on his famous horse, Traveler.

Veterans

The happiest most appreciative kindest people or I should have said men were the ex soldiers. My father and others who had gone through such hardships as cold, hunger, sickness, homesickness, heartaches and loss of beloved comrades, brothers some of them fathers. If it was snowing, sleeting or eastern gales, stormy etc my Dad after supper if in a talkative mood, would tell of the times they were on forced marches, men who wore beards and long hair very often had icicles hanging. He would tell of some occasions when they swam rivers when there was ice. How they slept out in the open when on these marches on the wet ground, sometimes when awakening being cover in snow etc. These men seemed so thankful for the simple things for homes, food and shelter.

They didn't seem greedy or grasping or fretful over minor things. They had suffered so and came through the fire as it were better men. Although I don't believe my Father ever got over his brothers deaths and he didn't like Jefferson Davis. My father loved the South and volunteered but he said after Davis and others knew the cause was lost and everyone else knew that they were overwhelmed. The North had the food, men, munitions, the South was completely beggared.

But the old Confederate leaders kept on and on and there was many precious lives sacrificed needlessly. Among them my fathers youngest brother only a lad of 19. During the war his widowed mother lost three sons.

My First Memories of Politics

It was in 1876, I was five years old when Wade Hampton was elected Governor of South Carolina. It seems our state had grown very tired of what was known as carpetbaggers and Negro rulers. I know the men in our community were at fever heat. I, being too small to understand anything political, only got thrilled over the groups of men running their horses up and down the roads with red flannel shirts on and their horse's bridles trimmed red streamers, shooting off pistols, hurrahing for Wade Hampton and giving the rebel yell.

Grandmother Alice's Necessities
Sealing wax, pencils, erasers, dip pens, fountain pen, Kodak, ink, Little Blue Books sold at newstands across the U.S. (1918-1952) Snow-Bound, Whittier, Sermon on the Mount, Wordsworth, etc. 3000 titles, printed 5 to 15 cents each. (Girard, Kans).

Chapter 6

My Father William Crain

My father, William Crain, was a devout Christian carried we children to church and Sunday School. He had an artistic nature. He would point out the wild flowers to us telling us the names of them also the trees and herbs, etc. He would take us out at night and point out all the stars and planets he knew and we would gaze and ask questions that he couldn't possibly answer. He taught me to love nature.

He had an eye for beauty even down to womens clothes. Could beat Ma selecting her own clothes. As she was practical, only viewed the heavens to speculate on the weather and that in relation to farming operations. No dreamer she.

He was no financier. What he lacked in financial he made up in kindness. He spent as he went but a more kind indulgent thoughtful father no one ever had. Instead of driving us he led us. When he wanted us to perform a task he would call us by name and say "Will you please do thus and so." I wasn't afraid of him in the least. No one in the world had a better daddy than I.

I remember as a child watching the spring of the year come in. Our fields were all fenced in with rails of chestnut wood eight to ten feet high. I would follow my Daddy to work and gather wild flowers, watch the birds and listen to their calls. These rail and also dead stumps had holes in them, knot holes and other wise. The blue birds come first and I did enjoy watching them clean out these places and see them carrying trash for them to live up to the time of feeding the birds.

In early spring the call of the turtle dove sounded. There

used to be more dead trees in the forest than now. It was a paradise for wood peckers with their rat-a-tat drilling a hole in the dead chestnuts for their nests. It was a comical sight to me to watch them standing on the side of the trees using their heads exactly like it was a hammer. In harvest time the bob whites were continually calling but owing to ruthless, heartless hunters they are most all gone.

In the dead of winter we could hear the lovely sound of the big owl calling hooo! hooo! others would answer hoo! hoo! They never failed to give me a chilly feeling. They sounded to me like souls. My dad said when they called, it was a sign of snow. All the time they hoo! hooted! in the bleak freezing weather and at night. They have passed too, to the limbs of almost forgotten things. There were also lots of whippoorwills. My estimate is that there used to be two birds where there is one now.

What I missed observing, Pa pointed out. He loved all the beauties of nature. I have seen him stop work lost in the wonder with a rapt expression on his face watching a beautiful sun set. He pointed out the moon rises and would carry us out at night to gaze at the stars to mediate and speculate on them. He wondered how far away they were, whether they were inhabited or not, never forgetting to tell us that God created it all. He would take us for walks in the woods, pointing out and telling us the names of different trees, shrubs and flowers. I don't think anyone ever appreciated creations more that he. He wanted everyone around him to be happy.

My parents were poor in this world's goods but were rich in kindness. They were both devout Christians. They both loved their neighbors, church and country. My father was a volunteer in the Confederate Army and served three years and four or five months. He was captured months before the war ended and was sent to a military prison in Indianapolis, Indiana.

He was five feet eleven inches tall and his average weight was one hundred and seventy-two or seventy-three pounds. When the war was declared he didn't know his own strength but the sickness, hardships and starvation and exposure left him almost a physical wreck. In about the year 1871 he was treated for heart trouble and couldn't work after coming from the war for a year.

He was never able at any time to do a full days work so that explains our poverty. I think the Rebel Yell must have been ringing in his head as long as he lived. He said the Yankees said they couldn't stand to hear it. He said his division would shout and holler to the top of their voices.

More About my Dad's Family

I only remember two of Pa's brothers, Uncle Jasper was the oldest. He was a red headed, keen blue eyed pepper pod, hot tempered fighting Christian. He was brutally frank, very generous, hospitable etc. When he was 18 years old, I think it was he entered a cotton mill in Augusta, Georgia, worked himself up in the cotton mill into some kind of boss position. He loved the work and stayed and stayed for years. In 1875 Col. Henry Hammett and others built a cotton mill and named it Piedmont. He must have known Uncle Jasper for he sent for him so in 1875 he and a man Jim Iler by name installed the machinery and started it. Uncle Jasper could have had Superintendents place but his health was failing so he took second place in the management.

He was thrice married. He first married a young lady Martha Coggins. Jasper and Martha joined the church Sept. 2, 1860. She died childless and also died young. I'm under the impression she died in one of the yellow fever epidemics that struck Augusta. Jasper had it once but recovered.

Sometime afterward he married a widow of Doctor Harris, Mrs. Mary Harris. She proved untrue. I think she was wealthy and lived an idle fast life. Anyway on scriptural grounds he divorced her. And the last time he married Nancy Prewette or Pruitt. She was a first cousin to his first wife.

While in Augusta he spoke to a Catholic Priest one morning. The priest did not answer so Uncle Jasper kicked him as he passed on by. His grandfather hated anything that was Catholic so the prejudice must have been passed on to the family. He was a mason a deacon in his church and I think he prayed in public, gave away nearly everything he made to charity, to his mother and I suspect he helped his mother-in-law who outlived her ten children and Uncle Jasper too by a good many years with Aunt Nan, Uncle Jasper's widow.

I remember distinctly going with Aunt Lizzie or Mother one to Highland to get the mail. Jim Wilson kept the post office, mail arriving there not more than once a week. I don't know, may have been once a month. Anyway Uncle Jasper wrote to his mother regularly. Nearly every time he would send a bill of money (One or two dollars) and the kind letters he wrote. It was,

"Now listen Mother, don't you and the girls do without anything you need".

And he would write saying,

"Mother if you need any money before you get another letter just let me know". Which she wouldn't do but this bought maybe a pair of shoes or coffee or taxes. Of course it was small amounts.

He spent all his vacations with his mother and when he broke down unable to work he left his home and stayed with his mother until he died. He must have been sick a year or more.

I remember the spot he sat on the front porch in summer. And when he bought or his friends sent him delicacies he would save some of them for me. I loved him dearly. He was so very kind. He was just as devoted to his mother as a boy 15 years usually is. And poor old Mother had to bury him too. He died either the 11th or 12th of February 1880. I was not quite nine years old but I have sweet memories of him. He was buried on the 13th of February 1880 in the family burying ground. He was 60 or 60 odd years old.

Uncle John was the next oldest. He moved West when a young man or rather he followed the railroads. He was the bridge builder. Sometimes he made his headquarters in Memphis, Tennessee. As a contractor he had to move. My father worked for him a while prior to the Civil War. At that time Uncle John had a crew of 90 men. He also said John was the brainiest, smartest one of their family. He didn't like farming but all the time scheming, planning and thinking of other things. He had a keen sense of humor. Being much older than my father, he was the leader in their mischief, practical jokes etc.

John L. Hawkins, Grandmother Alice's husband, also had a sense of humor . . . not always as apparent as it was on an occasion in the year 1910. Across from the front of their home on Ridge Road was a variety of fruit trees (apples, peaches, pears, and others). Sometime during the daylight hours he filled a lantern with kerosene and crossing the road he walked across an open field and entered the orchard at the greatest distance from the house. In the cover of the trees he moved back toward the house.

When he reached one of the largest apple trees he raised the glass of the lantern exposing the wick. With his free right hand he took a match out of his pocket struck it on the seat of his overalls and lit the lantern returning the glass to shield the flickering light. He climbed the tree and hung the lantern on one of the limbs that was visible from the house. Retracing his steps he returned to the house from the open field.

After supper when the dishes had been washed and the kitchen cleaned the family members became involved in various activities. Finally conditions were exactly right. It was a dark clear night with no moon shining. Granddad climbed the stairs and went to what I knew as my Uncle Cody's bedroom and looking out the window lo and behold across the road he saw the bright light of Halley's Comet.

He moved to the head of the stairs and called out in his loudest voice. I see Halley's Comet ! Halley's Comet ! Come on up! And they did every last one of them and there was a goodly number bumping into each other coming up the stairs. There it was! A comet only visible for one night every 76 years.

Some of those children who gazed out that window lived to see the real Halley's Comet when it appeared again in 1906.

Peddlar's Wares - Pattern, ribbons, laces, buttons, tin, embroidery hoop, and thread.

LEMON CHEESE CAKE
To Marcelle, the kind of cake your Daddy used to like when he was a boy.
1 cup of butter
1 1/2 cup of Sugar
3 cups of flour
2/3 cup sweet milk
1 teaspoonful baking powder
5 eggs
Bake batter quickly in layer pans.

FILLINGS
2 large lemons. grate rind and
    then extract juice
1 cup sugar
2 eggs
1 teaspoonful of butter
Mix butter, sugar, grated rind and juice of lemon then add eggs. Cook over slow fire, heat until well jellied. Place between layers and also on top of cake. Be careful not to burn as this filling scorches easily.

Chapter 7

The Peddlars Came

The people of my age and memory have lived to see more changes and more inventions than any other 60 years in a thousand previous years. We are now leaving the gourd era and now enter the tin peddlemans. Men used to go around in covered wagons peddling tinware. My Mother saved all clean cotton rags that were not used for wrapping bundles and sell them at the stores and the obliging tin peddlars would give one cent per pound.

It was an exciting time with me when the tin peddlar came. He was always in a wagon with bow frame and sheet as his bag of rags took a lot of space. He tied peck buckets gallon buckets half gallon quart cups pint cups were tied up and drawn all along the top ribs in bunches. And when he drove the rutted bumpy roads there was music in the air. The packs of dishpans, frying pans giving out a kind of clanking sound while the coffee pot, cups etc. gave out a tinkling sound.

These rags that were bought up were shipped to paper mills. I don't suppose wood fiber was invented and such sorry tin ware it had to be carefully dried after using as it was so bad to rust. I never heard of aluminum. Don't suppose it was in use. And there was not a cook stove in the community say in 1875. There was pots pans kettles tins to set the coffee pot on. There was the pot hooks to lift covers and lids with. There were tongs and shovel and the pot rack in back of chimney to hang the dinner pots on. There was usually a turkey or chicken wing fans to fan the fire with. These things were cut off the fowl whole and put on the hearth to cure and dry with a weight on

Tin pan, knife and cup

them.

When baking bread pies and so on the lid was placed on the fire to heat. Fire coals was placed under the oven. Then hot dough was placed in it the hot lid placed on top with live coals on it. So while cooking live coals were in demand and if oak bark or wood are used when cooking could hardly be done with other wood so to keep the fire booming the cook fanned and fanned much as a blacksmith uses a bellows. But despite the fact it was such tedious work such as stooping, lifting complexions burned smoked and grimed and no cold or cleansing cream. Smoking red eyes burned fingers it was the best bread in the world.

There was this peddlar who carried around pottery such as jugs churns crocks pitchers. As his load was noiseless I wasn't much interested in his load.

And we had the Irish peddlars who went all over the country periodically and Irish they being true sons of Erin. Usually two men together on foot who carried large bundles on their backs wrapped in oil cloth. Sometimes the bundles were so heavy they would look bow legged and always stooped it was so heavy and with knotted walking sticks to help them along. They were slow heavy red bearded blue eyed men who talked with a brogue usually sometimes a dark bearded one but invariably Irish.

These packs when opened up proved to be a veritable store of things such as scissors, razors, needles, thimbles, pocket knives, and pins, sometimes jewelry. Dress patterns so called because there was always cloth enough to make one dress.

This goods could not be bought in stores and was usually gay embroidered and when a girl dressed up in one she looked like she was from the steppes of Russia or the Balkans. He sold bandana hanker-chiefs dyed with turkey red that could be laundered with white clothes.

He carried Irish laces and embroidering lace made of linen thread. and beautiful Irish linen such as towels, table cloths etc. His cutlery was of the best English make as his dry goods were of Irish make. Nothing cheap or shoddy in that pack. The question is what became of him and his buddies? He seemed to have been like the Arab who folded his pack and stole away or was it a question of tariff?

When as a small child a man with his pack was seen coming toward the house Ma said, "There comes the man to take the census" and I became alarmed and had to have some explaining done. I thought she meant take our senses. I must have had an inferiority complex and knew then as I know now I had none to spare.

And there was the basket peddlar and her boys with their basket and sacks. Her name was Beck Wright. She would offer you a basket if you would fill it full of wheat, shelled corn or dried fruit.

And there was the trough digger. I don't suppose there was a metal wash tub in the world and wooden tubs with hickory hoops. If the tub got dry the hoops all dropped down. If it froze they burst off. So huge wooden troughs were dug, yes literally dug. A large yellow poplar tree was felled and the long log was sawed off and the the top of the log leveled off. There was a colored man in the community named Wash. I remember his digging a trough for us. He used a tool called an adze. It was like a maddock except the top had no axe to it. He kept that long narrow blade ground keen.

For a wash trough there was a partition with augur holes bored between it. It was a three partition of two and when placed on heavy logs of wood it was real convenient and was said to last for years. Some people had the same kind of troughs without partitions for soft lye soap. And some of the same soap was in the soap gourd on the wash shelf to wash hands and face which certainly came out clean and fairly shone after being scrubbed and dried on a home spun home woven towel as the linen towel was for guests.

Richmond College, Richmond, Va.

Post Card sent home from Richmond College, Richmond, VA in 1911. Back of card reads: *"Rc'd letter o.k. Very busy getting in shape for exams. Glee Club concert last night. Large crowd. Go to Forks Union Fri. to give concert. Does not seem like Xmas, weather is nice. No snow yet. Hope you are getting along fine."* **Allan**

Chapter 8

One of the Greatest Women

Mother as I called her was one of the greatest women. She was the strongest woman physically I ever knew. She insisted on having a small crop planted which Pa had plowed for her. Just she, Aunt Cynthia and Aunt Lizzie. She had corn, cotton, garden, two kinds of potatoes, indigo patch manufactured her own blue dye from the plant, a beautiful shade of blue dye from the plant, a beautiful shade of blue for both cotton and wool. She had sheep cattle hogs. Sheared this wool from the sheep backs. She would card, spin this wool and dye the blue with indigo, the dark brown was dyed with ripe black walnut hulls. The red-brown another shade was dyed with ripe black walnuts and leaves. I've forgotten what she dyed black wool with. Oh! I've just now thought. She had some black sheep.

She carded spun reeled this thread into hanks to be dyed. This was then wound off into quills which fitted into shuttles to be woven. This was called filling the warp, had to be cotton, had to be carded spun reeled into hanks dyed sized into starch put on swifts and wound off on the spinning wheels on to large spools, put into warping bars after forming what was known as a cross in the thread. This thread looked for all the world like a giant chain maybe 30 or 40 yard long and as wide as the cloth was intended to be usually 32 or 36 inches wide.

One end of this thread was spread out and rolled up on the thread beam. The other end of these threads were poked through a harness and then through a sley all the time preserving the cross. The treadle strings were fastened to this thread and then one mashed one treadle with the foot that thread opened itself evenly so there was space to throw the shuttle with the right hand catching it with the left, beating it with a batten one thread at a time.

A woman could weave 3 to 6 yards a day. It was such a tedious slow process but Mother finger picked her cotton, removed the seed with her fingers. She wove all or I should have said she and her daughters wove cotton dresses for everyday, underclothing, bed sheets, window curtains, counterpanes and in wool. They had wool dresses for winter, beautiful wool blankets, some pure white ones, some tan ones with blue and brown borders, etc.

She knit shoulder shawls which most elderly women wore in the winter every day. Mittens, gloves, stockings also spun sewing thread cotton of course. She dyed a lovely pink or old rose color with some kinds of herbs.

She made all the soap, dipped her own candles. In summer if she thought her corn was coming up short she would take a sack go to fence corners of the old garden places etc and would gather all the weeds she could carry to feed her hogs. She knew exactly what they liked and what was good for them. Those weeks with kitchen scraps, buttermilk and then feed them corn in the fall. Why, she raised her own meat.

It was very hard times. Not a sack of cotton seed meal in the world I don't suppose. In the winter she would shell her corn by hand pouring it into tight boxes and barrels. Keeping the cob she would take a hammer and break each cob into several pieces. Then when she had a large Dutch Oven would fill it full of those broken cobs have just enough water to steam them after covering them with a heavy lid. She steamed it about an hour as longer cooking hardened them. Those pieces of cobs would be soft and smelled good. Then she would throw in the quart or so of cotton seed which she had picked the night before, some corn meal and salt and this made two feeds for her milk cow. Her beef cattle had to content themselves with nubbings of corn and shucks. Well that cow would give delicious milk and butter also cottage cheese. I mean we made it.

> One type of a Dutch Oven was a metal utensil, open in
> the front, for roasting before an open fire. Another was
> a brick oven in which the walls are preheated for cooking.

When she butchered a beef she knew the part of the stomach called the rennet. She would dry some of it to use through the year. She would pass a slip of it through the milk. It would separate the whey from the curd she making it into delicious cottage cheese.

> When I was a preschooler our family lived at 50
> North Main Street in Greer. After supper mother would
> read out loud to us. Before beginning to read she would
> prepare oatmeal or cream of wheat in a fireless cooker.
> Oliver Twist by Charles Dickens was my favorite. Many
> a night I would live with young Oliver for a while and
> go to bed on the verge of tears if not actually crying.

> What is a fireless cooker? Food to be cooked is
> mixed and then placed in an insulated chest over very
> hot cast iron plate or plates. This is closed and in the
> morning oat meal or cream of wheat is ready to be served
> and eaten.

After Grandfather's death and her sons all gone most of her buildings went down. I remember distinctly her sheep pen where she fed them in winter. The lot was built of chestnut rails. She used a crook of the fence she laid sheeting planks, she laid it all over the top and she took a lot of pine tops laid them over tops and sides so it was as warm and snug. She had the same arrangement for some of her cattle. She could dig a hole set a post as well as any man.

She had a beautiful garden. Pa would plow it for her in the spring, all the cultivating was done with mattock and hoe. She had a pleasant walkway down through the middle with flowers. I can almost smell clove pinks, sweet williams, madonna lilies and others. She had sage lavender, rosemary and an herb she called comfrey. If one was unfortunate to develop a boil she would beat it up, it was mucilaginous and said to be very soothing. She had another herb she called elecampane. It was for hydrophobia and she said if one was bitten by a mad dog why you took the root, pounded it and cooked it in sweet milk the patient eating or drinking it as the case may be. We didn't test it out but we think it a faith cure.

In the corner of the garden were beds of Jerusalem artichokes which we children like to eat in the winter raw. She raised winter cabbage when the weather turned cold. She would dig trenches and set these cabbage just as close as they would set in rows, build a low rail pen around just above their head, lay plank over the top and used thick green pine tops over the top and sides. I've never yet seen cabbage so crisp and tender. She would set out some two or three best heads in the spring to go to seed. They would grow out and make seed. Dont suppose she ever bought a cabbage seed in her life or a beet or lettuce or bean or English pea seed in her life.

I wish you could have seen her winter stores of dried fruit in abundance both peaches and apples. Cornfield beans, table peas, meats, had plenty of chickens and eggs.

Sometimes in the Spring to economize on feed for her sheep she would say to me, "Come on Allie, lets get the sheep some feed." She would cut bundles of sassafras tops which had a yellow bloom and other things that were budding, give to her sheep, the sheep having already eaten as high as they could reach. That with a single handful of corn meal with a bit of salt made them a good meal.

When she dressed a mutton she would take the hide and tan it with the wool on as they were beautiful. The skin was soft and pliable. She would use them to throw over the bed foot on freezing nights. She bottomed some of her kitchen chairs wool side up of course. Mother had ready helpers in Aunt Cynthia and Aunt Lizzie. They did all the washing ironing, scrubbing, carried water up a hill, cooked over an open fire three meals a day and they kept the house spotlessly clean. In good weather worked in the open. She worked without fuss or feather, never seemed mad flurried or mad, had regular habits.

They didn't get up of mornings until daylight summer nor winter. Mother called it a day when working outside. She quit two hours by sun all chores done and supper eaten by sundown. In summertime we had our chairs in front yard where we could watch the day die and the stars come out. In winter they sat up late. Aunt Cynthia would knit or sew and mother would finger pick cotton talk about old times. Aunt Lizzie would tell me riddles, tell stories and sing and after I grew larger would sing and read aloud mostly the Bible and hymns. A weekly paper didn't last long.

Grandmother Crain remembered the earthquake of 1812. It played havoc in Tennesee and Miss. or would have if had been thickly settled. And there was the auroraboreales or northern lights of 1860 when one could see to read by it. And there was the comet of 1848. I heard these things referred to as a sign that the Civil War was coming. My Mother said in the North it would in changing colors look as red as blood. Not the comet, I mean the northern lights.

Well this all sounds as if I thought my ancestors saints but through the mist of years I only remember the best side of them. And if they were cranky or set in their ways which I guess they were I seem to have forgotten it.

It was reported and believed by my Great Aunts and Uncles that their father Great Grandfather William Crain had buried part of his gold and silver. In fact I think they hunted for it but failed to find any and there was a goodly bit to be divided. After his death I think they must have been mistaken because he spent quite a bit on his red headed brown eyed girls ordering or importing from England their finery such as silk etc. for their best dresses and they had the reputation of being well dressed and being very neat housekeepers.

Chapter 9

Today is March 12, l932.
Mother's Grief

It has been freezing cold about one week and at the present moment its snowing and one looks out on a mid-winter scene.

Some favorite Hymns
Just as I am without one plea
Holy. Holy. Holy.
Praise him praise Him
Doxology: Praise God from whom all
      blessings flow.
I need the every hour

October 22, 1930
What I Have so Often Experienced.

The clock is ticking, ticking, ticking and I am on my bed of pain, no rest, no sleep as the moon into the west is slipping and I turn over again. Hush mouse, hush your constant nibbling let silence reign.

I have written part of this in bed mistakes, scribblings, blots of ink and I'm afraid you will fail to read parts of it.

Mother said her mother, slaves and grandfathers slaves had to pick all the cotton used. It took a lot to furnish all clothing and bedclothing etc. It was called finger picking. Each Negro man had to fill his shoe full of seed. Women and children I mean one shoe before they were allowed to go to bed. She said it raised a lot of merriment among the Negroes if a fellow wore a number ten shoe. Meanwhile part of the Negro women would be carding and spinning. All worked until late bedtime.

This sounds as if I were an orphan and reared at Mothers. Well I stayed with them every bit of time I was allowed. There was a long time Pa would let me stay every other night. Ma got so sick of it she put her foot down and I was only allowed to stay one night in the week.

Mother would work all week and would attend church regularly. There wasn't any Sunday School in winter as we had no way to heat the church so there was no preaching service either unless the weather was mild. My Aunts would cook the dinner and she would read her well thumbed bible aloud to me before I was able to read for myself. She was educated in a private school by an Irishman and I don't know whether it was his brogue she picked up or not. Take the word ...have' she gave it the sound of ...hay', ...either' was ...ither', looked was pronounced in two syllables as were other words. She was a good reader but owing to her quaint pronunciation I listened to I don't remember what she read.

To have the financial means to send a member of the family to a private school gives us an indication of how they lived.

She got on alright when she was busy at something but Aunt Lizzie said she never ceased grieving over her sons and daughters who died, especially her soldier sons. She tried to keep it hidden.

When I was a very small girl, she thought too young to notice, she would walk past and I would follow her. She would wring her hands and cry softly. I asked Aunt Lizzie what the matter was. She said she was grieving over her dead.

Often I could hear her praying. I was not allowed to intrude. After she thought I noticed, in mild weather lots of times she would repair to the family burying ground and sit with her dead until it grew so dark, Aunt Lizzie would grow so uneasy she would watch for her. She was barely discernible. I would say, "Oh Mother aren't you afraid?" She would reply, "No honey, my dead are a lot of company and I love to sit with them".

She didn't have a grain of self-pity in her make up. She kept her troubles to herself but Aunt Lizzie knew. Grandfather left a clause in his will that if she would need any thing she could sell some land. I never did hear her say she had a hard time she never was known to mention selling land. She did her milling, cut what wood she didn't hire done, plowed her little crop, and was everything just like a son might have been to a mother.

When she was 80 years old if wood became scarce she would shoulder an axe, cut down a sapling and cut it into stick lengths. She died the 22 of April,1885 at the age of about 81.

P.S. In regard to Grandmother I have gone into details to give you an insight into the hardships the Confederate women and children had to undergo all over the south land. It was a case of root pie or die!

P.S. And the ones who were not industrious and resourceful were glad to work for a peck of corn a day, grown men and women at that.

You remember Uncle Shade so it is useless to describe him. I loved him dearly.

Aunt Lizzie. I loved Aunt Lizzie and I have never seen anyone show more love and more devotion to her mother than she did to hers and was so kind to me when I was a little girl that she was my favorite Aunt. She told me she learned to read in Sunday School .. they carried school books instead of Bibles, No schools yet.

Chapter 10

My Maternal Ancestors, The Mitchell Family

Thomas Mitchell (Great, Great, Great Grandfather) was an orphan eight years old when he was brought from England by a family by the name of Clark and was reared by them in Virginia. I know nothing of this family except George Mitchell, his son, left Virginia and came to North Carolina and from there to South Carolina moving to what is now the Wadely Barnette place in the Mountain View Section near Locust Hill Section. He moved sometimes in the 1750 to 1760 or sometime along there. As the county secured a concession from the Cherokee Indians about that time. He married Anah Dill. We don't know if he brought his wife with him or not, whether she was from Virginia or North Carolina.

My Uncle Ansel and his wife Marion on an examination of records found that Thomas Mitchell's wife, Anah Dill, was born in Kent County, Deleware.

Thomas, my Great-grandfather, who was the son of George, was thrice married by his 26th year. He first married Miss Godfrey. She died and he then married a Miss Barnette then there were two children, George and Hannah. His son, George died when a boy and Hannah died after reaching young womanhood. His third wife was Mary Ann Harbin, my Great-grandmother. She had six Williams in her family. If she needed someone she just called "William". To this union the following children were born: Duke, Elliott, William, Archibald, James,

Jefferson, Nancy, and Anah.

Thomas settled at the Mitchell old homeplace about 1800 or prior to 1800. He and his wife, Mary Anne, had a part in organizing Pleasant Hill Baptist Church. Great grandmother left the reputation of being a very pious peace loving Christian woman. Great Grandfather survived her by several years dying in the time of the Civil War.

Pleasant Hill Church is Organized

There were several families who met regularly for prayer meetings at their several homes. This went on for years, the only churches around being Tyger Baptist and Washington Baptist Churches. One day a man by the name of Barton said to be a very good man and worker in the prayer meetings, visited at the home of my Great Grandfather Thomas Mitchell. He called on Great Grandfather and Great Grandmother to tell them that he had a dream the night before that the community should organize a church. The dream made a hit and made them think about it.

It appears to me some of them could have had a day dream that a church was needed. I will state here that I am not one bit superstitious. I do not believe in dreams, signs or anything. Well the upshot was the brethern and sisters got busy and organized a church naming it Pleasant Hill as it was first built on a hill. It was organized in 1835. The first church was erected of logs near Great Grandfather Mitchell's home and near his spring. There was a gallery or section for slaves.

After 20 or 25 years it was moved near the present location in the corner of Gus Kemps field. I suppose it was a frame building but I have only a faint memory of it. Then a larger and better building was erected on the same grounds as the church now stands. Then a new larger and better one was erected thirty seven or thirty eight years ago. The seats were not comfortable and the building needed repainting. Money was collected for this. After it was reseated, repainted, etc. one preaching service was held. That Sunday night the Baptist Young People's Union held their meeting.

The same week, March 17, St. Patrick Day, there came a freak snow storm out of the North West, blowing down timber, out buildings and wrecked the church beyond repair. Now a committee is hustling around collecting money to rebuild. A brick church this time.

Perhaps insuring churches and homes was not a common practice at that time.

December 11, 1931

One of the kindest and most remarkable years to farmers I have ever remembered in our locality is dying. Crops all gathered, grain sowed and cotton all picked back in November. We had a bountiful crop of cherries peaches apples in fact all kinds of fruit. It has been too dry for vegetables except the early ones. No killing frosts, cotton green in the top and blooming up until December 8, when the thermometer suddenly dropped after a cool day, cloudy, blustery and suddenly turning into one of the heaviest sleet storms in forty years. The power lines are down, telephones, lights, radio's, etc. all out of commission, cotton fields are so dead as the Dodo.

The year 1932 was a

Grandpa John at Work

year of bank failures financial crashes etc. there will be an epidemic of hoarding and also and epidemic or robberies. It was dangerous to hoard money then and it is now.

Quilting Bee

The girls and women gave quiltings. They would get several quilts ready, have dinners and suppers. This custom went with the Civil War.

The young men began to gather toward night fall with fiddles and banjos. As the girls would finish a quilt a young man would grab it, wrap his favorite girl in it like a cocoon and his reward would be a kiss. Sometimes there would be footraces before hand. Oh such fun Pa said.

After a big supper of things like roast pork chicken pie pumpkin and sweet potato custards etc. the music and dancing and plays would begin. I heard this true story. There was what was known as a working in every poor home log rolling cotton pickings corn shuckings house raisings.

When a log house was built the neighbor men were called to assist. So at this poverty stricken home during the meal the husband piped up with "Susie (his wife) what did you put in your "tater custards"? They air the best I ever tasted. They taste like you had put sugar in them."

That was a short while after the Civil War. I don't suppose there was 25 pounds of sugar in Highland township at the time. Some of my relatives were there and heard the exclamation over the good custard. The South lay as poor stricken bleeding thing. That poor ex-Confederate soldier was so broken in health he didn't live long afterward.

More About My Maternal Ancestors

The first account I have of them was James Moore and his wife Keziah. My Great Grandfather Joseph Moore came from Grey Court, Laurens County. I suppose his father and their Grandmother a red Irish from the fact that he was dark and low and she a tall blond. He owned only enough land to keep his slaves busy of which he owned a good many. But which was not inherited by his children. They were freed before his estate was settled in time of Civil War. He was a boot and shoe maker also a carpenter. He was noted for his fine working, building log houses or tongue in a grooving or fitting the corners. He lived to be very, very old what I have been able to gather. He must have lived to be 90 or more years.

My Great Grandfather Crain was opposed to slavery and didn't own any. So were the Mitchell family opposed to it and also other men who were able to own them.

There was a severe economical upheaval in the South at the end of the four year Civil War. My grandmother does not dwell on this in her stories. After the devastation of lives during the years of war, her native state, South Carolina suffered in the transition from slave labor to nonslave. How did the farmer who owned slaves make the adjustment? Who worked the fields? Was he compensated for what was then his property?

Keziah Moore

Keziah Moore married Jefferson Mitchell. Grandmother Keziah was rather tall and straight as an Indian when young. She had a mass of yellow curly hair with brown eyes. Grandmother was dignified and didn't talk much to outsiders but was just as kind and loving with her family as could be.

Grandfather went to the Civil War, leaving her with six children. Of course they had stock, cattle and land but she had to pitch and make the crops during the four years he was gone.

She and the children worked in the fields in daytime, weather permitting. They would card and spin, knit and sew until late bedtime, that is she and the two oldest children. Only two were old enough to work at the outset of the war. Everything they ate and wore had to be made at home. Not withstanding all the hard work she said she would have almost starved if it hadn't been for Mr. Ignatius Few and his wife, a wealthy childless couple. He would send a Negro or Negroes with his oxen and cart and help get her winter wood etc.

Great Grandfather Thomas Mitchell was living with them but he was disabled by old age and disease. He could not assist them in any way.

I never in all my life heard Grandmother grumble about the hard time she had had or even talk about it. I learned about it from others. She was a typical pioneer who carried water up a hill and cooked the food by an open fireplace until she was an old woman. I noticed in her old days she had poor health. Grandmother had large capable hands that were always busy knitting, sewing, drying fruit, cooking etc., between sick spells.

She reached the early seventies. She sleeps in the Pleasant Hill Churchyard. This was the church she loved and supported as long as she lived. Her home was the preachers home and the latch hung on the outside of the door. She never seemed happier than when she was waiting on people. Not only my Grandmother, that was the way other wives and mothers of the Confederacy had to work and suffer, not to say anything of the many widows left with children.

Tongue nor pen will never record how they suffered loneliness, poverty and hardships. War is an awful thing I lived to see the results of the Civil War. The fruits of it were widowhood, mothers who mourned for sons who didn't return, poverty, and broken health. Lots of women I could remember never regained their health from having to perform mens tasks while husbands and sons were away in the Army.

Returning soldiers were nearly all broken in health. It finally all ended in a financial panic in 1873.

The World War I happen to know personally. The heartaches and horrors of it. It is not over at this date, October 22, 1931. There is financial panics, causing banks to break, unemployment, people walking the streets begging bread. Many factories are closed. It is estimated that six million people are out of jobs. All this is the result of war and the end in not in sight. Wheat is selling as low as 25 cents per bushel, cotton as low as five cents per pound. The present price is six cents per pound. Wouldn't it be a great thing if war could be out lawed.

All I've ever heard about Joseph is he was gruff outspoken and called a spade a spade. My grandmother, Keziah Mitchell, said when his Negroes were working in a large field in front of his home he would sit on the porch to watch them and if one stopped he would bang on his porch with a walking cane and they knew to go on.

She said when she grew old enough to spin, she was eleven years old, she would spend a week at a time at her Grandfathers. She said there were Negro women for every task so she wouldn't have to do anything but spin. Her father removed from Grey Court bought and settled on the place adjoining our place and belonging to the Wilson estate.

Great Aunt Anah Mitchell was never married. She lived to be seventy-two to three. She was very intelligent and well read. I was very fond of her and it was a treat for me to be with her. She had a good memory and was well informed. She was also a devout Christian. If I ever amounted to anything I owe it partly to her and her influence. She died in 1892 and was the last Charter Member of Pleasant Hill Church.

James Moore and his wife so far as I know only had two children, Joseph and Sarah. She married Tolliver Robertson a Baptist minister of note of Laurens County. Grandmother Keziah Mitchell during the Civil War was left with six children. Daddy Mitchell as he was too old and feeble to work, Aunt Anah, his old maid daughter lived with him. I mean the other way around. Grandma and the Children lived with them. Their lives were a repetition of Grandmother Crain during the war of work and privation.

Grandfather came home sick, Uncle Lum rode a mule to Greenville after him. He would ride a while and lie down on the side of the road, Uncle Lum walking. After finally reaching home he lay a long time a wasted skeleton, delirious at times had chronic diarrhea brought about by starvation. He used all his strength to reach home, so a collapse and delirium but he finally recovered and don't suppose he had another sickness until stricken with pneumonia only living one week. Will refer to his tombstone for dates of birth and death as I've forgotten.

FOUR GENERATIONS

1915 - Mary Anne, Alice, Alice and Alan

1942 - Alice, Alicia McCallister, Allan and John Hawkins

Chapter 11

Homes

One of the places of interest I call to mind is the Dr. Lister Place. Marcelle, he was your great, great, great grandfather. I visited there when a child, fifty years ago or more when Mrs. Margaret Lanford, his daughter (widowed daughter) who inherited it, lived in his old home. The outside rooms were falling to pieces then. It must have been in its time one of the best buildings in the country. I think some of the main part of the building is still standing.

There was one door had carving on the top, a sunburst or something. Then there is the Lister burying ground. I think you would enjoy investigating it and starting or keeping green your family history by writing it down for posterity.

Dr. Lister was very wealthy in the way of land and slaves. He must have owned a thousand acres of land on both sides of Tiger River. I suppose he was an original settler. You could tell by looking at the old buildings that somebody, smart and artistic, had lived there. I suppose he has been dead a hundred years or more. You see if there is a tombstone to his grave.

I think man who came to this wilderness that was only inhabited with Indians and wild animals and literally hewed out and founded a civilization deserve to have their memory kept green by their descendants.

Few Home

The William Few home was another interesting place. The Few Place is on the east side of Few's bridge on the top of the hill. It was a good house when I could first remember, large with inside walls of logs. Part of the old log walls of the house were still standing a year or two ago. William Few was a pioneer, reared a large family of Christian boys and girls. This house like the Crain house is toward 200 years old. The old family burying ground is near by as is the Crain burying ground, close by the old home.

Mitchell Home - 1895
Allan, Vernon, Alice, her mother - Mary Anne, her grandfather - Jefferson and grandmother Keziah, and Clementina Crain Mitchell. Separate kitchen is in back. *Notice the large brim and crown of hat.*

Mitchell Home

Then there was my Great Grandfather Mitchell's old home. The best I can learn it was built in 1780 or very near that. I know a remark Great Grandfather made about the deer being plentiful in this community up until 1800. In February of that year the snow drifted to the top of some of the cabin doors. It being so deep the deer bogged down and the hunters could pick them up. Even the forest has undergone a change since the last century.

Well, anyway he must have settled here when he first married. Some of the children, in fact several of the older ones were born before 1800. Anyway this Mitchell house, like the Crain house was well and substantially built of huge oak logs. The house was large with a fireplace six feet wide, roomy upstairs with a shed across the outside with two bed rooms in it. A large old fashioned kitchen was built separately from the big house with its wide fireplace and upstairs also.

Mitchell Home after John and Alice added the left side. Occupants: Granny Clementina, Allan, Granny Pa William Mitchell, Harper, Grandmother Alice, Ernestine, Ansel, Mary and Vernon.

There was the old clock standing on the shelf Great Grandfather built for it. It would talk in old timey clock language. It said tick tock, tick tock, just as slow. Even the clocks didn't tick as fast then as they do now. They were not geared that way.

This Great Grandfather died in time of the Civil War a very old man. These homes I have mentioned are all the ones I recall seeing that were built by original settlers. Most of the early settlers lived in log cabins that soon rotted down.

Our house was in use and was typical of one about like the bungalow. Ours was removed from the cabin class so much in use. My dad raised cotton, corn, rye, wheat. He was a good gardener. He had hogs, sheep, cattle, bees, etc. We had a fine orchard. There was scarcely any insect pests no Irish potato bugs no cotton boll weevil nor bean beetle no peach scale nor **the peach tree diseases.**

Author of *Grandmother Alice* supervises his Grandfather who is feeding the pigs.

Chapter 12

January 12, 1936 - Sunday
Church-Storms-Inventions

This beautiful Sabbath day my mind goes back over the years to my childhood days. I have not anything in sight only the the four walls and the really beautiful trees, grey, all bare of leaves, etched against a blue sky.

My first impressions of attending church which is not written in a fun making spirit. In our home I never heard in my life heard anything bearing on or thinking of a sacrilegious nature in regards to churches etc. and all I am or hope to be was instilled by just my parents and grandparents and this little flock of pious people if we did have a dear old preacher who served us a long time who took a different text each time but preached the same sermon.

Not only our little Baptist flock but we had a Methodist church hard by and Methodist neighbors who were God's noble men and women and who exerted just as strong influence on my life and was much better people than I'm afraid I'll ever reach as high a flame of Christian living as some of them did.

If this mild, sunny day had happened in the 1870's or 1880 we would all have attended church. There was no stove to warm by so by far the largest congregations we had were during the summer. There was no Ebenezer Welcome Church, no Baptist Church at Highland either so people came to Pleasant Hill walking but mostly riding horses and mules.

As a young child after the singing I would amuse myself by watching the people and listening. Sometimes I had my knees on the seat where my mother sat so I could look out. I can recall some of it as it all happened yesterday. Mules kicking at each other, cursing in mule language. When their heels couldn't reach their jug headed, wall eyed enemy, horses snickered hopefully for their masters. In the old country churches fifty years ago the preacher would pause and say,

"Brethren, there is a threat of rain. We will have a brief intermission long enough to bring your saddles inside." The saddles were rowed up in the back end of seats. Then the service could continue.

I do not remember a word of the long sermons. I remember the high pulpit. It was a boxed in affair entirely on the womens side of the church with an open space wide enough, after ascending two or three steps, for the preacher to squeeze through (on the men's side). If he was a tall minister it sometimes came waist high and if he was a small man his head didnt reach much above the book board. It was all as meaningless to me and was not half as interesting as a jack in a box.

One widow with a badly spoiled boy about my age attended church. He seemed to enjoy the service or at least kept quiet up to the time of prayer. The preacher knelt and was completely swallowed up from view so the boy in a high treble voice began — "Ma what is he doing? Ma why don't they sing?" sh hush from mother in sibilant whispers. "What's he talking about ma? What did he hide in that box fer?" It wasnt even funny to see especially after I saw his mother lead him out, break a switch and whip him. The little fellow cried piteously.

GINGER BREAD	A CAKE RECIPE I USED TO BAKE WHEN I WAS A GIRL:
1 tea cup molasses	3 cups of flour
2 cups sugar	4 eggs
1 tea cup butter & lard mixed	1 cup butter
1 tea cup butter milk	2 cups of sugar
5 tea cups of flour	1 cup of milk
4 eggs	2 teaspoonfuls baking powder
2 table spoons ginger	Flavor with nut meg
1 level teaspoonful soda	

June 12, 1936

Dear Son,

I have tried to give you an insight into how life was lived in the rural South in my childhood and for many years before which was handed down traditionally. Dear Old Aunt Anah Mitchell used to tell me stories about the Indians stealing white children. One case I have retained in memory.

The Indians raided a home where there was a little girl 2 1/2 years old. This child was captured and carried off leaving her mother heart broken. Some years passed and the whites made war on this tribe and recovered this girl and other white children who had been stolen. Word was sent to all near by white colonies to come get their children. There was a mother who ran down the row of children peering in their faces trying to identify her daughter. Finally she sat down on the ground and wept bitterly. The men who had these youngsters in charge told her to think back if there were games played or anything the child might remember. The mother happened to think of the song she rocked her to sleep by that she might remember. It went like this,

"Alone, no not alone am I in this wide world so dear I feel that God is always near."

So she started singing it. There was a glad cry from the now big girl the mother couldn't decide for certain was hers. She took that mother in her arms, it happened this bedtime song was the only memory left of her mother and home. This did not happen in South Carolina. These things really happened to the early colonists.

I've often thought of the horrors and hardships pioneers under-went, the fear of being tortured, scalped and sometimes the children shared the same fate as the grown ups. What high courage it took to leave civilization and settle among the Indians. Our Great Grandfather, William Crain did it. He settled right amongst the Cherokees and made friends and neighbors of them. They helped him in distress when his son Samuel was bitten by a mad dog.

> Wind in the trees
> Song of birds
> Call of the bob white
> Song of the whip-poor-will at dusk
> Bees droning
> A wagon passing,
> It only creaked and rattled,
> Didn't smell.

May 28, 1936

Some of the Leading Events of This Year up to Date

The electrocution of Bruno Richard Hauptman for the kidnapping and murder of Charles Lindberg Jr., twenty month old son of the noted flier. The huge dirigible Air Ship, the Van Hindenburg, the largest ship afloat has made two trips to America from Germany. The largest ship ever built in the history of the world, Queen Mary was launched yesterday. They expect to make the trip from England to New York in four days.

> *The Queen Mary served as a troop transport during World War II. After the war ended Margaret Benson and I were married. Her home town is Bottineau, ND. In 1965 our family of four boarded the Queen Mary in New York and she was our home for a few day on a trip to Europe. The Queen is now a museum moored alongside a pier at Long Beach, California.*

Local Happenings

Winter Storms of 1936

The winter of 1936 has been the roughest in years. There has been 8 snows and one snow storm, when the wind reached almost cyclonic strength. Thousands of feet of timber being blown down. This was the worst storm in our locality since 1845. That was in August but it came out of the North West too. That year nearly all large chestnuts trees were blown down. The blow lasted all day. My father was a ten year old boy. He said the chestnut trees that were left started dying.

At the present time I do not suppose there is one single chestnut tree left. The Chinquapins are gone too. Nearly all the original forest pines are gone and oak trees predominate. Untold millions of feet being cut and burned years ago that otherwise would still be here. Such a waste. Chinquapins grew in thickets on level land. Hills and Packs Mountain were covered in Chestnuts. This information came from Great Uncle William Mitchell.

Things That Outlived Their Usefulness

Things that were in use 75 years ago that outlived their usefulness or are entirely gone. Cooking utensils for an open fire pace, the pile of oak wood and oak bark near by to cook with. The pot rack built in back of chimney to hang the dinner pot on. The trivet to set coffee pot on. The turkey tail or chicken wing fan to fan the fire with along with the poker, shovel and tongs. The pot hooks, the long legged skillet to fry meat in, the large Dutch oven to bake bread in, the round skillet with long legs to cook corn meal mush in with some home ground grits was the only cereal used.

The strings of red pepper hanging from the joist. The bundle of bone set gathered for winter colds, sage for seasoning, a bunch of ditney to make tea. The dinner horn that hung beside the Kitchen door almost equaled the African Tom Toms. It not only brought the hungry men to dinner but was never blown except at meal time, unless in case of fire, sudden death etc. When the neighbors horns were also blown and the whole country side would be notified.

The bullet molds are gone along with the powder and shot horns the hunters carried. The flint piece of steel and punk for starting fires are gone. The spinning wheel is gone, also the cotton and wool cards. The loom with its ever web of cloth in it are gone as well as the warping bars to warp thread, the reel to hank thread, the bunches of thread stuck along in rows of the log kitchen. The basket of spools to work thread of the quills that were inserted in the shuttle to weave with. The Indigo dye pot that smelled so good. The ox cart, the pail that water was carried from the spring in, the piggin, a small pail, the soap gourd, the sugar gourd, green coffee gourd and then the gourd that held parched coffee ready go grind.

The bean seed gourd, coffee mill, and the gourd that held copperas to dye cotton cloth with to make britches. These were called copperas britches and were rather sneered at as they were made the cheapest way. The balls and hanks of knitting thread both wool and cotton. The blocks of wood called lasts as near like the human foot as possible, along with rounds of maple sawed, ready to make the shoe pegs to half sole the shoes. Some times the lasts were hard to remove from the shoe as those maple pegs were driven into it.

June 1, 1936

This year so far has been unusual. It began in January. We had eight snows, some deep ones climaxed by a snow storm, with cyclonic proportions as has already been written. Then on April 9th or tenth a terrible storm hit Gainesville, Georgia. It was twin funnel shaped twisters killing a lot of people and tearing down buildings. This June 3rd haven't had dust settled by rain but once a small shower since April 10th. Cotton nor corn not planted on some farms and where it is planted there is hardly any up. We had a fairly good grain crop.

Hiram Crain was in here today and said there would be seven years of it. I predicted he would hear thunder and be dodging lightning in a weeks time. And lo and behold it rained last night, a heavy shower. The men are out planting cotton this morning.

This is a scene many saw as they passed
along Ridge Road in the early days. As far back as
I can remember Henry Carson worked for my
Grandfather. During the many years of active
farming Henry was ever present. After the fields were
'laid by' for the last time Henry continued to live in
the small white house just south of the homeplace.
This is still his home. After farming operations ceased
he was custodian for many years at Skyland Grade
School. He was a good friend of all.

Chapter 13

June 4, 1936
Old Fashioned Country Doctor

We were all taught to beware of night air, it was considered so unhealthy. Why, I do not know. Every window and door was closed at night on retiring. Heavy underwear was worn during the winter months. Some old men wore red flannel underwear. The women invariably wore heavy wool petticoats, red flannel or balmorals. Balmorals were heavy, woolen, wide home woven petticoats. Men and women wore wool stockings. I notice people don't die any faster now than they did when swathed in woolens.

There was the old fashioned country doctor who rode horseback with his saddle bags on the saddle behind. He carried babies in one side and medicine in the other.

Yes, babies. My wife said her sister came the same way in North Dakota in 1920. She saw the doctor walk into their house with his satchel from his car.

There was Doctor Caldwell at Gowansville, Doctor Wood at Tigerville and my Uncle Doctor J. W. Mitchell. My uncle who rode a very large horse named Doctor Knott who paced along at a rocking gate after Uncle John attended a patient and Knotts head was turned toward home he could sleep in the saddle. Uncle John did most of his sleeping in the saddle.

My world didn't have any germs or vitamins. It was a

case of follow your nose or appetite. We did have a mixed diet from the fact we tired of one thing and demanded something different but not for healths sake.

The babies then were not fed cereals on the farm as they are served today. There was rice and the crumb of corn and wheat bread, milk, butter and pot liker or liquor. In some families new born babies (not in ours) the first nourishment was a plug of fat bacon stuck in his mouth, the why I don't know.

Well, anyway the babies had never a taste of orange juice as no one saw any except a few at Christmas and as tomatoes only grew around the back yard or out on the hog lot fence and they were small and sometimes bitter and were not in general use so there was no tomato juice. I don't know where the vitamins came from. Larger children ate raw turnips, raw sweet potatoes and chewed and ate dried fruit and raw cabbage and stalks. And there were just as many rosy cheeked boys and girls as there is now and they lived as long.

There were old people, some lived to be 90 and older. Their diet of pork, beef, mutton and dried fruits and two kinds of potatoes seemed to agree with them. The thrifty housewife had a store of dried apples, peaches, damson plums, dried blackberries, pumpkin and figs. And people who were thrifty kept bees and stored enough honey for winter.

The Bees Swarm

I did enjoy watching the bees swarm but enjoyed the antics the older people cut better. There was a plow hanging on a long string and a cowbell with a stick to beat them with. Some beat in addition a tin pan. Some would throw dirt into the air and holler pandemonium would reign until those bees settled or got into their heads to go to the mountains.

My Father and Mother were both quiet and gentle until

the bees swarmed and to see them turned into howling savages beating tom tom's would excite me almost beyond endurance. I wonder if that was necessary. There was a superstitution abroad that if the husband or wife died someone had to go to the bee yard and tell the bees. And called it telling the bees or the bees would do no good. My parents were not superstigs. When I say bee yard I mean bee yard. As cattle, hogs and sheep roamed the country at will the bees had to be fenced in too.

The men folks had a hard time keeping up fences hog tight. And another hardship as there was nothing known about building soil and no fertilizer used, why new grounds were cleared fences moved and that soil cultivated until the soil was exhausted and let lie two or three years to rest all of which required lots of fencing of chestnut rails as wire fencing had never been dreamed of.

I distinctly remember the neighborhood cattle would frequently go in gangs, also hogs and sheep and the clanging of cow bells and tinkling of the sheep bells so all the family had marks for cattle and hogs. Notches in their ears and round holes punched. All calves pigs etc. received these marks while young and helpless.

What New Things I Have Seen

I don't suppose there was a home can of fruit in the state of South Carolina nor a teaspoonful of peanut butter in the world, no chocolate, no mayonnaise dressing nor a layer cake in Highland township. The old ladies of my acquaintance baked solid either pound or sponge cake and this was usually done either at Christmas or weddings as sugar was in the luxury class.

I've seen electricity come into use, the telephone, the sewing machine these were just coming into use when I was a small girl and caused lots of talk and excitement amongst the neighbor women. They were named the Wheeler and Wilson, that is the first I saw were and a woman would walk several miles to get the hem stitched in her best dress or to have the top of her sun bonnet quilted and considered a mark of distinction.

Same about cook stoves. I've a very dim memory of Grandma Mitchell. It was an Iron King she owned the first one in the community. It was made of good material. It was cooked on for 40 years and maybe in use yet so far as I know.

The first startling invention was the bicycle. I remember some of the men folk on returning from Greenville say he saw a man riding on a contraption that looked like his old spinning wheel except it had a little wheel rolling on behind. I fail to know when they first come into use unless it was about 1880.

After that we saw them in Greenville men on them wearing derby hats and the horses were afraid of them.

P. S. I forgot to say buggies were never as plentiful as automobiles are today even after rubber tired ones came in that was considered the last thing in luxury. They were called the fine new buggy.

Did the buggy get its name because some fellow decided it looked like a giant insect? Buggies had high wheels, ox carts had huge high wheels, wagons have high wheels. Don't know the motive unless it was so they could run over stumps in the roads. There were low stumps in some of them.

Jan. 8, 1935

The plow stocks were all homemade of wood. I never saw what was called a goose neck hoe until I was a good sized girl. One eyed hoes were heavy awkward things. The plow lines were spun and twisted at home. My first spinning was thread to make plow lines which Pa and Uncle Shade made on a contraption (I forgot its name) Uncle Shade owned and they helped each other make this rope.

My dad when a boy had his shoes made as did the rest

of the family. The shoes were made at home out of leather Grandfather had tanned. He said there was a Spaniard used to go to their house staying for days. When finishing he would pack his tools to other homes.

Well when I was a child our shoes were funny high topped affairs with a shoe cap on the toe to keep us from scuffing them out. Pa did all the shoe mending, cutting shoe strings of leather. Instead of tacks he used wooden pegs. He made them of maple wood with much sawing it into rounds, seasoning it and take his shoe or pocket knife place it on this wood. Giving it a light tap. He would finally reduce it all into a heap of pegs the right length and size to fit the pegging and holes and then tapping those pegs and strange to say it held the half sole on firmly. And in winter with my home knit wool stockings sometimes these were brown red but mostly striped.

Usually I was equipped for the weather and usually a thick woolen petticoat home woven that reached from neck to below the knees and home woven wool dresses known as linsey because it was soft material. And when bedtime came sink down deep into a feather bed with home woven woolen blankets and we didn't suffer from cold. I don't remember, I expect we suffered from heat as every door and window was closed as everybody knew night air was unhealthy. All the folks I knew were afraid of it and I was about grown before I ever knew anyone to venture to open a window.

FOUR GENERATIONS
1947 - John, Meredith, Reese and Allan

Chapter 14

Roads and Trip to Greenville

How roads were built in South Carolina in the late 1870's and 1880's. There was a law that each able bodied man between certain ages had to work a number of days each year on the roads. One of the men acted as overseer. I suppose he spotted the nearest patch of young pines or the flattest limbs of the larger ones. If you should have happen to see this group this is what you would have seen. You would have met a fellow driving a mule wearing a collar made of corn shucks hitched to a wooden plow stock which resembled a giant grasshopper with a shovel or twister plow opening the ditch on either side of the road.

Look coming out of the old field maybe ten or twelve men carrying all the pines, some holding them aloft, some dragging them. These pines were placed in the low places etc. Then dirt was shoveled on them. Well, you can't imagine those roads, so narrow, wagons couldn't pass each other on a hill. They had to accommodate each other by waiting on the edge of a field or a level place. Sometimes stumps were flattened still standing in these roads, sometimes field stones were poured into the worst holes. The result was that in wet weather muddy water would squirt over the team and wagon and in dry weather dust.

When you started in a wagon anywhere it was rattle, bump, squeak and jerk. Sometimes the wheel would sink down so quickly and unexpectedly that it would almost unjoint their necks. Sometime in winter the red mud would be almost hub deep and in going uphill the occupants of the wagon would all jump out, get behind the wagon and push. No wonder a trip to the Court House as Greenville was called took 3 days.That is, if the roads were muddy and the days short.

Coffee Kettles Coffee pots frying pans etc. would be used. There was and, oh the poor victims of sick headache, hence the coffee consumed. There was not a restaurant in Greenville and the first time I heard one mentioned they said there was a place in Greenville called Rest Your Ant.

It was a pathetic sight to see a mountain wagon pass, the poor fellow headed for home prostrated with sick headache. His feet stuck up with lines wrapped around them, the lines over his neck and shoulders, vomiting over the sides of the wagon.

Along about 1877 Pa and Uncle Shade decided they would go to the Court House to buy a sack apiece of something called guanner. Twas said to make the cotton grow so they went down and invested in a bag apiece. They headed gaily for the mountains.

Pa said after two or three miles on their way home they both became sick. Pa said he never smelt the like in all his life. They would take time about vomiting. Pa said he thought his head would burst before he could get home. They stayed sick all the way home. Pa put his sack of guanner in a cotton house out from the dwelling, but it wasn't long until the guanner scent penetrated the house. I believe I remember the name of the bag Wando. It must have proved effective because it wasn't long until the use of commercial fertilizer increased. Later chemicals were mixed with it to kill the odor.

Coffee Cup

Sometimes guano was put in the cotton row with horn made of tin and sometimes a substitute of poplar bark was twisted into shape like a huge horn of plenty or a giant trumpet. The victim carried a satchel over one shoulder and fed it by handfuls. The horn kept it from blowing away. Finally some smart alec invented a glorified wheel barrow. It was rolled by hand and was quite an improvement over the horn. I don't think there was any fertilizer used in this country prior to the Civil War.

Your father Vernon informed me, after writing about the guano, it was from Peru and he says the buzzards would follow the wagons. Some of the old timers who didn't quite get the name guanner called it 'doo anner'.

At that time there were not any terraces no legumes no county agents no two horse plows no mowing machines no spiked tooth harrows and no grain binders. Great grandfather Crain cut his grain with a scythe and threshed it with his horses and oxen, tramped it out on a threshing floor and its progress, progress. My father cut his grain with a cradle.

The farming operations were carried on this way, bottom land for corn and a piece of new ground for wheat. After a field was cultivated for a few years it was pronounced worn out. The field in time provided a lot of young pines to work the roads with.

After Thoughts

Greenville county in the dead and gone years had a whipping post for minor crimes. A chain gang had never been dreamed of. A lawyer was not allowed to go into the court room to plead for his client.

Pa went to Greenville once or twice a year. If he had good luck maybe he would reach as far as Milford Church by noon or a little below Sandy Flat. He would stop and make a fire and make hot coffee. Greenville was hardly ever reached the first day if the days were short.

He and Ma would begin making preparations the day

before. She would boil a cut of ham (pa didn't like fried meat on the road). She would bake cake and ginger bread, dried fruit pies etc. She would parch and grind an extra amount of coffee, put in a kettle and add blankets or quilts. This was all loaded in the wagon the night before. Pa would add an axe to the wagon and adjust the bow frame and sheet.

They would get up before day and light out on the 18 mile journey. There was a mile stone near home which said 18 miles to Greenville, S.C. I should have said a slab of wood painted white and those mile posts were set a mile apart all the way to Greenville and the Rutherford Road as it was then known carried you up hill and down dale and spilled you into Rutherford street.

I wish you moderns could take a trip exactly Iike I had to Greenville when a child of six or seven years. I begged Pa until he let me go. The roads were so narrow that two wagons couldn't pass only in wide spaces. There were holes a foot deep that wagon lurched squeaked and protested all the way down. By starting from home before day we reached Morgans lot to camp. I forgot to say when men worked the roads they filled rocks into the ruts and cut and toted green pine tops into the worst mud holes.

We camped in Morgans wagon lot. Pa stopped before Taylors took out his axe and went into Joe Edwards woods (I've heard since he owned 1800 acres along the road). He left me in the wagon went into the woods, chopped some dry oak and some fat pine to build his fire to boil coffee and to sit around. Lots of the people only reached 3 mile spring but that night I never knew what the word 'tired' meant before. I was exhausted.

Morgans lot was maybe 1/2 or 3/4 of an acre fenced in and had a big gate. The planks were set up and down and on the inside were built good substantial feed boxes a convenience and there were rings I think to hitch the horses to. Back to the wood and pine, any traveler who camped along the roads cut wood and pine wherever he pleased as no one seemed to care.

After Pa secured his fuel the next I remember was seeing the old farmers squatted around the fire talking laughing joking smoking chewing, some of them sitting in chairs which they had sat in coming in. Nothing unusual to see a man and his wife sitting side and side in chairs in their wagons.

The next I remember was the horses chewing, stomping gnawing the fence once in a while. A mule drown everything out into a loud bay squealing kicking sidewise at each other. The smell of smoke, frying bacon and the odor of coffee. The next I remember Pa laid some bundles of fodder in the wagon for a pillow spreading the bedclothes over it. That was the last I knew until next morning. I awakened to the hubbub of feeding horses and roosters crowing in every direction (course crow and shrill ones). Every family in Greenville must have kept chickens and never before or since have I ever heard the like. The scene closes. That is all I remember of this trip.

I forgot to say these wagons had a frying pan holder on the side and was very much in evidence. A lot of times when a man wanted to pay his taxes he rode horseback from our community and more people rode horse back to church than any other way. The roads were so rough. The old woman could mount her horse on her side saddle, first of course donning her long riding skirt which reached almost to the ground, take the baby in her lap, maybe from one to three children on behind her.

When reaching their destination there was what was known as a horse block for the women to alight on. She would unbutton that long skirt and wiggle out of it while alighting as she was so hobbled she couldn't have walked a step with it on. The men were right gallant looking from the knees down. They nearly all wore boots and had shiny spurs buckled around the boot heels.

Cooking in Fire Places

I've seen this occur. Preaching services during a revival was held at early candle light when a small child. All I got out of those services was the singing and the swirl of insects around these candles. There were all sorts and sizes of insects and critters that came through those unscreened doors and windows and ever so often a candle would be blotted out. My grandfather Jeffy Mitchell would arise in his tip-toeing, dignified manner and light that candle with another candle. Out would go another one to be repeated. Poor fellow, he didn't own a single match. If that congregation had been searched, its pockets turned wrong side out it wouldn't have revealed a single match.

All cooking was done on fire places. With oak wood and bark being used. Some fire could usually be found in each home but sometimes we borrowed fire and we loaned fire.

Chimney

Most of the old stick and dirt chimneys were out when I was growing up. I only saw two or three in our community. Nearly all the chimneys in use were that kind when the country was first settled. They were built by taking lengths of split wood and building a pen only it had a chimney shape. It was then daubed and plastered with mud. If the thing caught on fire I think a strong man with a piece of timber could have pushed it down.

If you had taken dinner with a friend and after reaching home some of the family had asked what was served for dinner and if you had mentioned iced tea or ice cream they wouldn't have know what in the world you were talking about. Spring water was the coldest thing in summer available. I do not suppose there were a half dozen wells in Highland township. Water turned on in house by a spigot by electric pump from ones own well as we have now had not been dreamed of.

Well progress kept progressing until there was a well at most houses. A long stride in relieving drudgery of the overworked farm women. The well was just about as good as she wanted, still not dreaming of running water in her house.

The first cook stove was marvelous. Grandmother Mitchell bought the first one in our settlement. I remember standing looking at the strange contraption. She was the envy of the whole community. It wasn't many years until all the most well to do bought them.

The Donahoo Family owned the first sewing machine. I remember the neighbors would carry their dresses to them and hire them to stitch the hems of their dresses and sun bonnet tops. Well in another decade sewing machines became plentiful. The sewing machine called for spool thread, so it was progress, progress. One invention called for something else.

There were absolutely no ready made clothes for women or children so fashions didn't change so often as now.

View of homeplace from side yard.

Chapter 15

The Country Stores and Remedies

In the late 1870's or 1880's there were two up to date country stores in reach of us, Wilson's country store and the Reese country store. There were wrappings and containers for groceries and dry goods. As you entered the door there was a counter and near the front door a show case. In the show case there were knives, buttons, needles, ribbon, hooks and eyes etc.

Shoes and boots in the store were in large wooded boxes, large enough (if my memory serves me right and I know I am not far wrong) to hold eight or ten bushels of grain each pair tied together by its own strings. Boots (and there were a lot of them worn) tied with twine through the straps that they were pulled on by. There were boots, Brogan shoes, women's polkas, little boys boots, little girls shoes all thrown together higgledy piggledy with the merchant on one side and the customer pawing through until suited.

I can't recall if they were laced up. Since they were tied together I don't believe the merchant wrapped them. Being tied together they could be conveniently carried across the arm or saddle horn. I do not suppose there was a paper shoe box in the world. My everyday shoes had a brass cap on the toe to keep them from scuffing out.

In the row with the shoe box the merchant had a keg of horse shoes, a keg of horse shoe nails. On the wall hung bridles, trace chains, collars, all kinds of things for plowing and hauling etc. On the other side would be a box of western bacon and somewhere a barrel of brown sugar, usually furtherest from

**Window display of a country store;
union suits, stocking and cap.**

the door as every man and boy black and white would help himself to a handful of that crumbly brown sugar and eat it. Don't remember ever seeing granulated sugar.

There were no tubs or buckets of lard. I don't recall seeing a bucket of lard until I grew up. There were no sacks of flour. Flour was shipped in wooden barrels of two hundred pounds. I suppose that gave it the name of barrel of flour as these barrels held 200 pounds.

And there was a kind of cracker that come in paper lined barrels which also stood open and there was the barrel of molasses with its measuring cups and funnel. No syrup in buckets or cans hadn't been invented. And the western bacon was about all that would look familiar in a store today. Coffee was sold green and was shipped in large crocus sacks. It had to be parched and ground at home. It was wrapped in stiff brown paper and tied with paper twine (paper twisted into twine) which was surprisingly strong if it didn't get wet. There were no paper bags. If there were they were not used in the south.

There were no cans on the shelf except axle grease in tin boxes and was used on iron axles. The wooden axle used tar.

If you had asked for a box of matches he would have handed you a small elongated wooden box with lid on it and I don't know how many matches it contained, any where from one dozen to 18 and they were 10 cents a box and matches were not in general use but a rare commodity. If the fire went out some kind neighbor gave you a start. One was usually in a hurry when borrowing fire hense the old saying if you made a pop call you surely came to get a chunk of fire.

If you walked into a store and asked to buy a can of tomatoes, a box of chewing gum, bran flakes, a box each of puffed wheat and rice, tooth paste, mixed soup etc. etc. why the merchant would know by that time you were insane and it was time to tie you up. I can't recall a thing that came in tin cans except axle grease and sardines and scarcely anything in paper boxes.

Hats were some elaborate creations. So many plumes ribbons flowers and sometimes streamers they had to be taken care of. Some of them looked like huge bouquets and they were lovely to look at. But I now know that placed on the heads of the average sunburned flat large footed farm girl will leave you to guess how out of place.

And there was the matter of dress goods. Most women were wearing homespun clothes every day but for the best beau the manufactured cloth. And after buying 10 to 15 yards for dress the merchant usually threw in a spool of thread, a card of buttons and maybe hooks and eyes gratis.

And for the men there was grey blue brown and mixed jeans (course fabrics) which sold three yards for one dollar as homemade jeans was fast going out by the time I was ten years old. The good housewife could get a pair of trousers out of three yards. Buy three yards of ordinary sheeting 28 inches wide would take those sharp scissors of hers fashion them into garment the like of which I wish you could see.

She made his trousers with pleats down the outside seam, no hip pockets and unless he happened to be an old fashioned cranky fogy, his shirt was buttoned up the back. He

Galoshes or one-buckle overshoe for boys.

very often had to call on his good wife to button him up. If the day was warm and if he was knocking about as he called loafing, gossiping and whittling topped with his flat crowned black straw hat he didn't look one bit funny to us.

The stores were run by men, a lady clerk was unheard of. The only edibles sold out side of bacon, sugar, rice, New Orleans Molasses was cheese crackers and sardines.

I forgot to say that these stores carried heaps of leather for sale. Each man was to mend the shoes for his family and he did it with wooden lasts whittled out of a block of wood. The last was slipped into the shoe and held firmly between the knees. The holes were made through the leather with an awl. It was pegged on with homemade wooden pegs. Sometimes these pegs would go too far into the pegged holes and stick Pa. He would turn red into the face and sometimes I would get uneasy afraid I would lose my hold on the shoe as the leather was pegged to it. In a few years someone invented an iron last on a standard and iron tacks. But now shoes are rarely mended at home.

There was plug tobacco for sale. It came in wooden

boxes something like octagon soap came in a few years ago and the green country swains called it manufac. I don't think there were any cigarettes and cigars were as scarce as hens teeth. Homemade twist reposed in almost all the jeans trousers. There wasn't much smoking among the men because there was no way to carry fire around with them. So most of them indulged in smokes at home.

I used to follow my dad around when very small. He would sometimes start off smoking this pipe, became absent minded thinking of something else and let his pipe go out. He would draw fast on the stem part and work at the bowl of his pipe. If it hadn't gone entirely out it would revive and he would with a satisfied look resume his walk.

If you had walked into a store and asked to buy some garden seed the merchant would have stared at you in blank amazement. The country woman raised her own garden seed as she could replenish from some obliging neighbor and lots of times she named them after the neighbor. My Susie beans, beets and cabbage etc.

All these seeds were hung up in little cloth bags and when she divided with her neighbor it was tied up in a budget old scraps of cloth having been washed and saved for that purpose. These little budgets looked exactly like the money budgets our Uncle Sam of U. S. A. is pictured carrying. And if the neighbor was scarce of butter in the summer time you gave it to her wrapped in a cabbage leaf.

No butter paper	No paper napkins
No cellophane	No paper bags
No paper cups	No paper plates

Hardly any paper boxes that could be used for carrying purposes.

The hunter carried his shot and powder in cow horns slung over his shoulder, with a leather strap packed down his load with a wooden stick known as a ram, packing a clean rag over shot and powder to keep them from spilling out. The caps were carried in a small metal container. And when he shot at a fleeing rabbit with a single barrel gun, why Mr. Rabbit could be in the next township while he was reloading.

Every well furnished kitchen had a flour barrel and meal barrel, also a coffee mill. It was said now that the world lives out of paper bags. Back then the world lived out of barrels.

Mornings I used to sleep, I used to sleep until the process of cooking breakfast and the coffee was ground. The coffee mill raised such a chatter that it awakened everyone from Grandpa to the baby, as done the last thing before breakfast. And the coffee was never boiled long enough to turn the ground coffee over a time or two in the pot as boiling water was used in the making and it was set aside only long enough to settle. With freshly roasted and ground coffee it far exceeded coffees of today.

June 1, 1936
Some Home Remedies Before the Civil War.

Bleeding was practiced in all sickness. Grandfather Dennis Crain had a lancet and neighbors went to him to be bled. A pain was blistered with Spanish flies, terrible blisters that took a long time to heal. Calomel and more Calomel rhubarb, aloes were used. Hot foot baths, boneset, red pepper, ginger and tea was the remedy for colds. In typhoid and childbed fever no water or practically no water was allowed. The fever parched victims.

There were no dentists and when a patient developed a gaging toothache, if the tooth didn't burst (No, I am not joking, they sometimes did) the poison went into the jaw easing the tooth some. A victim of jaw ache was unsightly.

Back in the winter when the house wife cooked a jowl she saved the jaw bone (not the kind of jaw bone that Samson of old testament fame slew a thousand men with) but a hog. She cracked this bone scraped out the marrow and greased

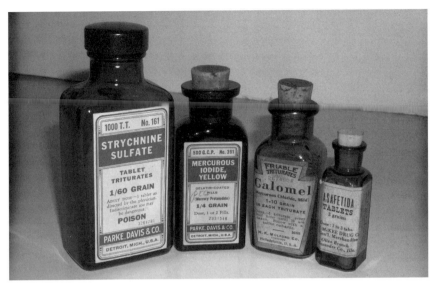

Old Drugs

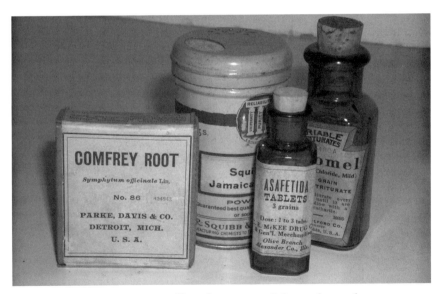

Home Remedies from an old cupboard.

the poor aching jaw. I suppose it was effective as no deaths were reported. The greased jaw then took on a shiny red slick appearance. A twisted wool cord tied around the waist to ward off cramp.

A brass ring on the finger kept off rheumatism. A set of Mole's teeth worn around a babys neck made teething easy. A pill of asafetida worn around the neck kept off contagious diseases.

A ceremony by certain people took off warts. Nails were dropped into a vessel of vinegar and allowed to rust. This was taken in the spring time as an iron tonic. If one stepped on a nail one went out during the summer gathering an herb, called plantain, bruised it and applied it to the wound. If a mad dog bit you, you stewed elecampane root in sweet milk and drank it — very effective. Some remedies.

If one looked pale was copperas pills. Still good. Sulphur and molasses was used for a spring tonic. Some made tonics of dogwood, wild cherry, poplar and other barks.Whiskey was added and he called it bitters. When a fellow announced he had sore throat his mother would stew the inside of red oak bark or make some green sage tea with alum in it for him to gargle.

We lived in a world that had no germs, no vitamins. The world lived in blissful ignorance of the fact that he had an appendix much less one that needed removing. He didn't dream of having tonsils that were polluting his blood stream. He knew nothing of flat feet, halitosis or B. O. etc.

Appendicitis killed people then but was known as cramp colic. There was no ether or chloroform, no hospitals, no dentists. In extreme cases a hammer and nail was used to knock out an aching tooth.

Progress in Traveling

My Great Grandfather Crain carried his hogsheads of tobacco to market on trucks rolled to Charleston, South Carolina. My Grandfather went to market at the same place and Hamburg, S.C. in a wooden two horse wagon. The wooden axles required an application of tar instead of grease. If in need or tar it set up a loud squeaking, the wagoner resorted to the ever ready tar bucket which dangled on the tongue on the back of every wagon. These buckets smelled good but that was all that could be said in their favor.

Well anyway I do not know how long it took Great Grandfather William to make the round trip to Charleston but it took Grandfather Dennis a week to go to Hamburg. He went one time every year. He bought a barrel of New Orleans molasses, a sack of green coffee, tea and other incidentals. The balance of his supplies were home made.

I notice the difference in the time and what a contrast in traveling when you and your Dad went to Florida. You reached Augusta, Georgia by noon in your automobile. Hamburg doesn't exist now. Don't you suppose the next generation will be shot down in rockets in a few minutes?

I had better say for Marcelle's benefit that Hamburg, South Carolina was opposite Augusta, Georgia. The town is no more. I do not know why unless it was washed away. It was on a river and was the market for the whole upper country. Indians and whites visited this market.

From Candle Light to Electricity

It would look strange now to modern eyes to see torch light processions leaving the churches at night. I do not suppose there was a lantern in Highland township. Here in the March of Progress, since I can remember in the last fifty years, the church and homes were lighted with candles until I was about ten or twelve years old. Then my daddy bought a brass lamp. It was a jug shaped affair, held a pint of Kerosene and had a wick in the top about the size of a lead pencil. We were deathly afraid of it and well we might be as the gasoline had not been separated from the Kerosene and it proved it wouldn't mix with fire.

In about ten years after that some body invented brackets to set lamps on the wall in and then some smart alec conceived the idea of swinging them on a chain. Up to this time, September 1931, we have installed electric lights. I have an electric light bulb hanging over me right now. What next? It is in the lap of the gods, unthought of by mortals like me. What is to be next?

More Medical Remedies

I forgot to say a tar kiln was part of the equipment of every regulated farm and, OH! how good they smelled when in operation. The tar was used as a medicine also. Some people kept a dab in their water. They smeared it on their horse troughs, wore it on their backs and chests as a plaster. It was considered almost a king cure all. Well come to think of it, it was about as innocent a thing as they could have pinned their faith on. That reminds me of some more of the homely remedies practiced among some of the people.

A pint of bone set tea and a dose of salts taken before retiring was supposed to cure a cold. It induced perspiration and it really did. The patient didn't stop at gentle perspiration, he sweated. The proverbial mole had nothing on a victim full of hot bone set tea. It was a whole lot better remedy, than to wear a pill of asafetida around the neck as a preventative or to nail a horse shoe over the door. Some buried a sassafras pole in the path where the witch passed so as to break the spell she cast on the neighbor's cow, causing her to give bloody milk (mastitis). It would take a well filled book to tell of the practices, beliefs and language used by our mountain people.

Where the People Settled

Up until fifty years ago, our Glassy Mountain was much more settled than now. It is said the people kept much of the language and customs, handed down from Queen Elizabeth's time.

They used old hymns and sang through their noses. They had old time fiddlers and banjo pickers who couldn't read one word and didn't know one note from another. They had their arts and crafts and managed to wrest a living where a goat could hardly stand up. I suppose the most of the mountain people were Scotch Irish, the Barton family were. Other large families were Pruitts, Howards, Ballews, Gosnells, Durhams, Ross's, Bowers, Harts, Pittmans, Lindsays and others. It seems the mountains were settled before the Flatwoods as they called our community.

Mountain People

These people were said to retain largely the language and customs of Queen Elizabeth time they being fine English stock and they must have had some of the same patterns for their clothes strange cuts and gay colors and ruffles looked like some of Charles Dickens characters.

About the year 1876 they started out of the mountains to the cotton mills until no one lived there since. In our community it seemed the people followed the streams. There was lots of fish and game and they planted the bottom land in corn. They not only had plenty of fish and game but also had wild turkey and deer.

Chapter 16

Church Life

Mules in Church Yard

Well I'll say when a large congregation met at church for a funeral or a union meeting or association there was enough horses and mules to carry on a stock show. And around the churches were saplings drooping tree limbs beside hitching racks. Many has been the times when the preacher would get warmed up and reach a high note. Why, some mule would cut loose bray, not to say anything about of the stamping, fighting flies, nickering and sometimes an especially lively one would break loose and around the church they would go head up and tail up, kicking at the others trying to cause some more to break loose which they would.

The old men would usually carefully remove their saddles sticking them under the church floor or up in the crotch of a tree or by the root of a tree. But some of the young careless men would hitch their mounts with saddle on and when one got loose I have seen the stirrup almost stick up in the air and such a clatter.

Those things were such a common occurrence when the preacher was drowned out or when a horse struck out lickety split for home leaving his master afoot miles from home. No one seemed to think it funny. Why the modern preacher couldn't conduct a service now under such circumstances..

My parents were pious devoted Christians. When there was services at our church I went too from the time I could remember. We only had two services a month for years and years. It was held the second Saturday of each month and the Sunday following. So I employed my time, when not asleep, watching.

Some of it I can remember better than what occurred yesterday. I didn't seem to have a soul or any conscience. If I had it hadn't developed. I guess from my 4 to 8 or tenth year I was only an onlooker. Hadn't developed a sense of humor either, just took it all as a matter of course.

I can see now the Amen Corner. Especially the Amen Corner set aside for the women. The men had a Amen Corner too on Saturday 11 o'clock meeting, especially in the fall of the year when the good housewives had been dying wool and cotton preparatory to making the winter jeans etc. This stuff had to be dyed when the walnuts, barks, herbs etc had accumulated all the summers sun as the sap was stronger and refined. The preacher would arise in the pulpit announce a hymn, maybe blood is the road that leads to death or hark from the tomb, a doleful sound etc. He would read out two lines, the people arise to sing and he'd line out two more down to the last.

But if you could have seen those wide long skirted sunbonneted aproned women with their large knuckled bony capable hands primly crossed on their stomachs. These same hands some of them as brown as walnut juice could make them as far up their sleeves as I could see, some as blue as the bluest thing you ever saw, some of them as yellow as a buttercup, some of them a lovely pink, some a dark red and some purple and some matted with mited edges. They would arise with all kind of voices issuing from those sunbonnets. They usually swayed as they sang giving inspiration to their long home made jeans. Well, if it could only be put on a stage no one would believe they would say it was so overdrawn no modern would believe.

Jean is a sturdy twilled fabric usually of cotton.

Ginger Bread in Church

Well my mother, before kneeling, had given me a piece of ginger bread to try and keep me still. No doubt I stood up on the bench that time watching Aunt Carrie who was sitting on an empty bench behind us. Well Aunt Carrie spied my ginger bread and began slipping along the bench whispering and motioning. I don't know whether she took the bread or whether I handed it over. She slipped back against the other end of the seat, leaned her back against the wall and with a bland self satisfied, "I've reached the height of my ambition" expression, proceeded to consume my ginger bread. I wasn't surprised only stared in open mouth astonishment for her nose met, I mean her chin met her nose every time she chewed.

If my mother had known what was going on it wouldn't have been necessary to have kept that firm grip on my leg next to her or a handful of my skirt which she usually did to keep me still. I watched until the last crumb was consumed. I didn't forget it and after I grew old I asked my mother what it meant, a grown woman taking my ginger bread. She told me the lady had an only son, a good fellow unmarried, the pride of his father's heart, idolized by his mother.

He enlisted in the Confederate Army and was killed. His father died and Aunt Carrie grieved so I think a kind providence said it's enough and dethroned her reason, but not her taste for ginger bread. Mother said she would sit up in church and watch. If the mothers gave their children anything to eat she would get up to join them and say out loud, "Honey, give me a little bite".

Marcelle, I guess there is a lot said about ginger bread and not cake. Child, after the Civil War sugar was scarce as hens teeth and sold high. Money was scarce and the sugar was brown sugar. I do not believe granulated sugar was in use. My mother and all the neighbors baked ginger bread. They used eggs, butter, ginger and home made syrup. They baked it in thick pones and stirred it when it grew cold. Now I am the

Aunt Carrie of the community and like a pone of ginger bread (no not ginger cookies) better than any Chocolate cake or any other cake for that matter.

A Five Cent Silver Piece

I forgot to tell you about one very good intelligent man who I expect was eighty years old or more. Well, he was called upon to lead in prayer in a revival meeting. As I said before, when everyone was on their knees was my time to arise and watch. The old fellow knelt in the aisle in front of the pulpit. He prayed a while, cried a while and then turned it all into a laugh, one haw haw after another weaving on his knees laughing and the tears running.

I remember asking after that what he thought was so funny. They informed me it was the Holy laugh and I confess that to this day I don't know what the Holy laugh is or was. Lets whisper it low. I expect the old gentleman had hysterics. I looked under the table and benches for something funny to laugh about but didn't see a thing let me say here I was not nearly as surprised as my elders. It was all a jungle of meaningless words and actions anyway.

Ma told me as I grew older, Grand Dad Jeffy Mitchell, with his ever quick thinking said "Amen" and assisted the kind old gentleman to his seat. He was Ignatius Few, a wealthy high toned, Christian gentleman in every sense of the word. A pillar of Fews Chapel Methodist Church. He was childless. His wife died years before he did. He was beloved by his relatives and neighbors. He died in the late 1880's. Ansel, he gave your father John L. Hawkins his first piece of money, a five cent silver piece.

*Grandmother's daughter, Helen Hawkins
Forrester, heard her Papa tell about Mr. Few giving him
the first piece of money he ever owned. He told the story
over and over as long as he lived. It was one of his
happiest memories.*

When I was a girl growing up we had never heard of Irish potato beetles or cotton boll Wevils. Called by our colored brothers and sisters "tater bugs, bean beegles and cotton boll evils."

Church Meetings

When the revival or 'big meeting' held annually in August, after the preacher had carried out the first service in the morning he would announce the next service to be held in early candle light. It was. There would be two or three candles burning on the wall on either side of the pulpit and one on the book board for the minister.

I remember we always walked to church at night. We had a trail through the woods. All heads of the family if the moon was not shinning, prepared torches of light wood, split into pieces about a foot to eighteen inches long. When the fathers reached the church, they would stick the torch wood under the floor until time to start back.

I do not recall any of the service except the singing. My mother bedded me down on her big white and black shawl until time to start home. I shall never forget the lighting of the torches and the journey home. I enjoyed seeing those torches leaving the church in every direction. There were four family parties who traveled over our trail. The path being narrow we traveled in sheep fashion each father carrying his torch over his head. As he was taller I can see Pa now the weird red light reflecting on his face with the stream of black smoke trailing behind. Sometimes the hot tar would drop on the hands of the bearer and they would burst into profanity, seeming to forget the sermon they had just listened to.

I would clutch my mothers hand and wrap in part of that wide skirt to keep from getting behind and we would both walk in the same skirt as it were and there was room for two or three more of us. I was afraid of the dark (and I'm still afraid).

There is one thing I didn't like at church was about we poor dust crawling worms of the earth. I didn't like to be compared to a worm. Then there is a hymn <u>Why did He devote that sacred head for such a worm as I.</u> I didn't like it then and I don't like it now.

But my day meeting was something to be enjoyed. Ma had a little black satchel and before leaving home she would put slices of cake or ginger bread to feed her starving child. She had a pretty white quart cream pitcher she carried along stopping at Hiram Crains Spring filling it with water to quench the thirst induced by the eats she was all armed to hear the sermon and join in the singing which she enjoyed so much. I was in good trim to watch the proceeding.

When we would arrive at the church there would be usually groups of men sitting and standing around talking, chewing tobacco and talking about crops, politics etc. Sunday School was supposed to be held at 9:30 o'clock and preaching at 11:00 o'clock as folks observed A.M. time and there was no one to keep correct except by sunrise or sunset, getting the time out of the almanac so the folk consequently had different times.

Anyway the women after lugging and dragging the babies to Church were glad enough to go into the Church to sit down after the men had waited for the congregation to gather. Some man usually Uncle Jim Mitchell who happened to own a hymnal book would come in and whistle a tune, a signal for the fold to come in. Sunday School would proceed. Each one would carry bibles. The classes sat in a row and read a chapter (which had been selected last Sunday), reading her part out loud until the end of chapter had been reached. Some teachers would comment on the chapter and some couldn't think of one word to add to the reading. There were several classes some reading Job or Psalms. Matthew. No organization. A song or two would be sung (with no musical instrument) and some old Deacon would get up and announce,

"Brethren we will now have an intermission of 15 minutes" (which by that time was sadly needed). The folks would pour out the door the young folks making for the spring. It may not have been intentional but it beat any matrimonial beginning in starting a romance. The girls might start to the spring alone only to be escorted back by some rural swain.

The preacher would ascend into the pulpit, would read his text saying,

"Brethren lets all jine in singing hymns number so and so. Why he announced the number except for the benefit of 2 or 3 ladies I don't know, as there wasn't but one, two or three hymn books in the congregation. The preacher would read in somberous tones. A typical song, Broad is the road that leads to death and many enter there. A pause. The congregation picks it and sings it. A pause. But wisdom shows a narrow path with here and there a believer. All sing again.

Brethren lets pray the preacher says. The whole congregation plumping down on their knees with the preacher sunk down out of sight in his pulpit. I amused myself looking at the row of shoes turned up. Some times they had been newly mended with white wooden pegs, some two rows and some one row and some little bunches in the middle.

One old fellow was fat and he had a ready made frock coat which was split up the back to the waist. It was buttoned up and had pockets inserted in each to take his handkerchief. He was very careful with the coat and when he sat down he would look on either side bringing the skirts forward and placing them over each knee. So when kneeling he would arrange it in front of him so his lower back stuck up behind in what would be a funny way now. I only remember it. And when prayer was being offered there were responses from the brethren aloud as Yea Lord!, do Lord! and some would utter deep groans as, Ugh-ahoo.

Well, anyway this old gentleman referred to above who owned the long black coat especially designed for ministers was called on to preach one day and the weather being very hot he had left said coat in the vestibule. So he walked out donned that long coat, pranced down the aisle into the pulpit.

We had another dear old brother with a thick red beard. He fascinated me. (My Dad didn't wear one.) The old fellow dearly loved to sing and I would watch the contractions of that red beard. When he would feel especially happy he would turn his face up to the ceiling. I discovered he had a neck. He was an attentive listener to the sermon, he stroked that red beard all the time with an up and down motion and if the minister said something of which he approved or disapproved, I don't know which, he would close in on that beard with his right hand as if he meant to pull the whole thing out. I would watch him to see how much he would get at one yank, then he would only release it to go on stroking. I wouldn't be at all surprised if he had pulled his whiskers out.

Another old lady was very cross-eyed. She would get enthused at what the preacher was saying, lean one elbow on her knee, push back her bonnet, one eye on the preacher and one eye on me.

There was another dear old couple who became tired of the benches and carried a chair apiece to sit in. I suppose those two chairs occupied two of the choicest locations for 20 or 25 years. It was a childless couple and sometimes during these intermissions a stranger would plump down into the chair on the mens side. His wife would watch that chair like a hawk and when the congregation was settled she would walk over and say out loud, "You will have to get up, this chair belongs to Pa."

One day the old lady went out at intermission. Meanwhile a very plucky woman in the community with a fretful baby sat in her chair and she was swaying back and forth. Well, when the lady returned after intermission she stepped right over to her and said out loud, "Get out of my chair". The woman in the chair said out loud calling her by name, "All right, I'll get out this time but it will be the last time I will move for you."

We had a preacher who preached for our church for years who wore his hair long. He had a cowlick or a contrary lock which insisted on falling down over his eyes and all I remember getting out of his service was to watch him smooth it back in place. When the first time he nodded or shook his head down it came again.

And there was two or three dear old sisters who shouted, scaring me out of my wits. I did the weeping while they did the shouting. My mother would lead me gently out. You know old mother nature is the gentlest most soothing thing I know. When I would get out, see the trees all still and all nature hushed, why my emotions settled at once.

There was one of our brethren, a reformed drunkard, he had a crooked nose no doubt the result of some of his drunken scrapes. He had a clean shaven face with the exception of a bunch of whiskers on the end of a sharp chin. This beard was allowed to grow 5 or 6 inches and then was cut square. He had a very expressive face and sometimes preached. He was of a highly emotional nature and I don't think I'd ever heard him preach without crying so. I'd watch that goatee, sometime it would be drawn around sidewise and sometimes it would stick straight out in front. After preaching would be over he would come out of the pulpit shake hands around and maybe join in a laugh. I remember how I wondered how he ever stopped crying.

And another thing I believe or was lead to believe by their prayers that they were filled up with the things they prayed for and all in the world they had to do was open their lips and let the words flow and when he happened to look my way I wondered if he could see us.

Sometimes the sermon would be well under way when

Clothes the 'stylish dressed woman' may have worn.

the preacher would call a halt by saying,

"Brethren I believe we are going to have a rain so you all can feel at liberty to take in your saddles." They would row them in the back of Church and some would have them under the floor. They would come in resume seats, the minister picking up the broken threads of his discourse.

Storage under the floor was possible because the building was supported on piles with wide space between them. In the early days I suppose these supports were of wood or stones. I know our house in Greer was supported by brick piles. We had ready access to a play area under the house. In modern constructions that have concrete base building codes require termite treatment prior to pouring the cement.

But this actually happened too. There was a door for the men and one for the women. It so happened there was a man and his wife from another locality, she a beautiful woman stylishly dressed came in at the mens door with her husband. I heard such remarks as "Did you see that brazen thing come in at the mens door." Well, you know, I expect I was 50 years old before I ever ventured in at that door which is more convenient than the other sometimes.

I believe those Saturday meetings were held on purpose to keep the brethren and sisters straightened out (those primitive people didn't have a thing to do but watch and listen to gossip) so from a child to the present I've noticed it invariably stirred up hard feelings. For instance if one good sister talked about another she was brought promptly before the Church.

I remember one old man was visiting one Sunday and someone cut a gash in his overcoat. The old one hauled the other one into the Church. The brethren tried to get him to own which he wouldn't and he would deny it every time. Well the elderly gentleman who fought so spitefully had that young man turned out of the church after getting it all split into factions. And they worried along for months. I was large enough by that time to resolve if my feelings were hurt I would never, never carry it to a Church.

There were no newspapers except a little sheet in Greenville called the Greenville Mountaineer. Very few took that. No movies, no magazines, no radios, no automobiles so I believe all the trouble was brought about by excitement and something to feed their minds on. Most of the cases were laid into the Church by the grouchiest, longest faced, I mean blue looking people we had.

We had an old lady in the Church would literally raise the D.......... in the community. I heard her say myself in bad inclimate weather, "No where to go, Nothing to talk about". Then she would ride over the settlement and (tell a certain old lady who refused to allow anyone to talk about her) a big tale about her enemy had told her, pass on and tell the other old lady the same. Said she would have fun. Then it almost equaled a cat fight.

The men were not so hard up for amusement. They (I mean the gambling element) would have what was known as Gander pulling. They would select an old gander. It was supposed to have the toughest neck of anything that was harmless. They would take it and tie its feet securely to an overhanging limb if a tree the right height for a man on a horse to reach it. The rule was to whip his horse to top speed and the man who succeeded in pulling its head off won the circus.

Also they had shooting matches. Tying a turkey on the ground in some manner and standing off a long way took shots at it. The one shooting it in the head got the bird. And all these fellows if they happened to be a Church member was yanked up and out if he didn't say he was sorry and ask the Church for forgiveness only to repeat the offense.

When Sunbonnet Meets Sunbonnet
In speaking of some of the women of the church.

"I wish you could have seen them as I did. Most all of the elderly wore aprons long wide ones. The material was all the way from home spun cloth to black silk. Each old lady if it was summertime would have a bunch of spearmint, peppermint or ditney stick in her apron bands. If it was winter it would be allspice, cinnamon bark or ginger stuck in pockets. Cinnamon bark could be bought for ten cents a bunch. They would nibble on these things industriously through the services or through a gossipy conversation before the service began, when sunbonnet met sunbonnet, resulting in complete isolation from curious outsiders. A sunbonnet extended fully five or six inches before the face with a skirt filled."

Chapter 17

Hog Drovers and Funerals

Chestnuts and 'Soo Cow'

There were lots of chestnuts in this part of the country, Chinquapins grew in thickets. The hogs ran wild and fattened on Chestnuts, Chinquapins and acorns. This food was called mass, why I do not know.

The homes and cultivated land were all fenced in, cows, hogs and sheep ran wild. As a child, I remember learning the different cow and sheep bells. Each flock of sheep had what was known as a bellwether. It was usually the gentlest sheep or cow that wore the bell.

If a housewife could hear the tinkly of her cow bell in the distance she would stand and yodel Soo cow, Soo cow at the top of her voice. As a child I could hear them in different directions. The house wives didn't need voice lessons, some of them could be heard a mile away, and sometimes, strange to say, if these cows didn't want to go home they would go to the deepest, darkest thicket in the woods and stand still to keep their bells from ringing.

As to the hogs each family in the community had its mark, so many notches in the ear, sometimes holes were punched in their ears or tails cut off. Each man knew his mark. The calves were marked the same way as the hogs when very young.

In about the 1879, a law was passed called the no fence law. It was reversed. Fences were built for the cattle instead of fences for the homes and crops.

Hog Drovers

When I was a small girl each family killed and cured its own supply of meats at home, even the folks in cities butchered their own. We lived on the road known as Gap Creek also the Rutherford forked at or close to the Gap Creek leading to Hendersonville and down to Gap Creek was driven droves of horses, mostly mules from Tennessee and Kentucky which was Oh such a thrilling sight!

Two or three fine young men, booted spurred and fine saddled riding usually fine horses and all these mules followed sans bridle or anything. My mother had such a horror of us being caught in the road and maybe yet get run over and killed as mothers are afraid of automobiles.

But what I started out to tell was about the droves of hogs. Of course they had to be driven in the coldest and sometimes roughest weather of winter. These hogs were raised in Ohio, Kentucky and Tennessee and were destined for Greenville, Columbia and Charleston, South Carolina and into Georgia as the best way out of the mountains was the Cumberland Gap.

In 1828 the livestock (horses, cattle, sheep and hogs) passing through this gap was valued at $1,167,000 and in 1824 something over an estimated million dollars passed through Saluda Gap. I have a notion some of the stuff was shipped to Europe via Savannah, Georgia and Charleston, South Carolina.

There were men who built mule, cattle and hog pens along the way. They kept the drovers in what they called Inns. The Dickeys at Highland had pens for the cattle and ran an Inn for the drovers.

We would get so excited on hearing a drove of hogs coming. Of a still morning we could hear the chorus a mile or two away I mean the hog drovers as it was such slow traveling. There would be several drovers each one would have from 50 to 100 head to be responsible for. They would be dressed in Western cowboy style, wide hat, tall boots and red bandanna or grey scarf around their neck. The drovers carried long black snack whips. They would almost play tunes with them over the hogs backs.

Those fat hogs traveled at a snail pace rocked from side to side sometimes belly deep in red mud. The drovers rocked along coming down in almost the same tracks talking hog language, coo'ee, hoo'ee which they seemed to understand. Sometimes the drovers had the appearance of slipping up and down in the same place. Sheep and turkeys were driven also but I didn't see them. Three and a half or four miles a day was considered a good days journey to the next feeding station.

The way those hogs were managed by their hog growers (as they ran wild) was to raise some at home and gentle them and when the wild ones were caught their eye lids were tacked together with needle and thread. The gentle ones served as leaders.The wild ones would follow the grunting and snuffing to their destinations.

The hog drovers were considered a romantic figure amongst the young ladies. There was a ballard sung amongst themselves like:

Hog drovers, hog drovers, hog drovers we air.
A courting your ladies so young and so fair.
Can we get lodging here, Oh here,
Can we get lodging here?

It was said the drovers only received a wage of $ 15.00 per month and when he sold out had to walk back home. It took a fast walker to walk 33 miles a day. So has passed from this country a picturesque figure except on the pages of history, never to return.

Then and Now Grusome but True

There was not an Undertaker in Greenville County, if there were they didn't undertake in our vicinity. There were not many ready made coffins, a few upstairs in furniture stores and none when I can first remember. Coffins were made by carpenters and covered in black cloth lined inside with bleaching or white cambric. Some of these coffins had handles, some didn't and these were carried by hand sticks. Four men usually bore the burden on these sticks. Pall bearers were not chosen but were usually sturdy men who were accustomed to it.

I shall never forget Grand Dad Mitchell's face helping to turn those sticks through a narrow door. He would purse his lips and turn his mouth one sided with a look of Oh! I'm so afraid we will let it slip. He had the appearance of being in pain. After the corpse was viewed I remember hearing hammering. I consulted older ones. Some said the box was nailed down. There were ropes or leather lines to lower the coffins into the graves. Some coffins were slipped into a tomb, a shape hewed out of the red clay to fit the coffin.

The last funeral I attended without benefit of undertaker, I stayed in the church during internment. A small boy ran in saying, "Mrs. Hawkins, the lines broke and let it drop."

After death a wake was held and still is. When I was growing up the young people would gather and some older men too with their hymn books, they would sing and this was interspersed with eating and drinking coffee, giggles, flirting, etc. In some places twas said they would sing all night quartets, duets, etc. It mattered not how the poor pitiful victims had suffered or how tired, worn and sleepless the family. It was the custom and custom prevailed.

The funeral lots of time was held at the grave side consisting of a hymn or two a prayer and the poor makeship of a coffin let down with plow lines. Well that was not the end of it though after the simple short service usually by

Grandfather Mitchell, why maybe 6 months later there would be the 'funeral' the former called a 'berrying'. Well the preachin at funeral meant for all the clan to gather attired in deep mourning occupying the front seats funeral hymns such as (and must this body etc, etc. die, this mortal frame decay) etc.

The preacher would talk a great deal on the virtues of the deceased, never mentioning any of their vices (just as my ancestors are lauded by me).

As there were no daily papers, phones, or radio prior to the Civil War. My Father went for a visit to his brother Jasper in Augusta, GA. There was an epidemic, he heard about, of yellow fever. The people were dying like flies when he arrived. A man died that day near where Uncle Jasper lived. Pa said it was almost impossible to get anyone to sit up with the dead. He said he was awakened sometime in the night by a duet singing, There is a fountain filled with blood. One man and one woman was all that sat up and they were singing. What a blessing mortuaries.

There was a young man who went to Texas from our church and married. His young wife soon died. In a heartbroken manner wrote back that he wanted her funeral at Pleasant Hill Church.

Well a Sunday was set, his friends and family met at the church. I shall never forget, brother A. D. Bowers said he felt handicapped as he nor the congregation didn't know the deceased except what the bereaved husband had written about her. He said she was the best woman in Texas or the world for that matter.

A sauce to be poured over and eaten on dried peach pies, either baked or fried tarts.

> 1 short pint of sweet milk
> 2 egg yolks
> 2 tablespoons of sugar

Milk eggs, sugar all well beaten and cooked in top of double boiler, stirring constantly until reaching the consistency of cream. Flavor with vanilla.

Chapter 18

The Lowly Gourd and Log Rolling

First there was the lowly gourd. To begin with it grew around the horse lot, cowpen fence anywhere the soil was rich and it looked as if it was sent by divine providence and filled a need.

Most every barn yard had a long pole erected with cross arms with say a dozen gourds tied securely on for birds to build their nest in called martins and they were called martin gourds. These martins were supposed to keep the hawks away and these would return year after year and build.

P. S. Another receptacle to keep salt in. The men would saw a section off a hollow black or blue gum tree, nailed plank over one end and stood it on end and it was as smooth as silk on inside and the bag of salt would be emptied into it and it was called the salt gum.

Part gourds played. There were different shapes and sized, some were dippers used to drink water. They had a long handle that stuck up out of the water bucket. I have a distinct memory of our old fashioned kitchen with shelves on either side. One side next the back door has a pail, a piggin pail was a home made article made like a tub. A stave on each side came up longer with holes bored and then a piece of rope tied through to carry it by. My Dad had gone modern and there were water buckets or two on the long shelf and we toted water what would be now considered a long way. And I was Chief Water Carrier for a long time. My brother helping me.

Aunt Elizabeth better known as Aunt Lizzie had acquired the art learned from the Indians of carrying a pail of water on her head without touching it and would also carry smaller vessels in either hand. I used to go with her to the spring and back up the hill behind her just to watch her straight back and graceful stride.

Well as soon as I became old enough I began carrying things on my head without holding niddling and nodding and weaving from side to side and spilling water down my back. I finally learned to carry it as well as Aunt Lizzie.

On the other side of our kitchen was shelves and nearly all the containers were gourds. The kind that had a bottom and sat on the shelves, round brown and fat looking with their necks cut off, and stoppers with clean rags around them for the ones that held edibles. There was the one for salt, coffee, sugar, lard and soft soap. For the dye stuffs, copperas and madder and blue stone for the wheat.

These gourds grew and ran on horse lot fence, anywhere as live stock wouldn't eat them as they were extremely bitter as were the vines and unfit to use until soaked scraped and boiled. And the drinking gourds were frequently boiled in clean soap suds.

One of my aunts owned one as large or larger than a peck measure she filled with green coffee after getting a hint of the blockade in time of the Civil War she kept it for sickness and drank substitutes corn, rye, wheat, and okra seed and had some of it left when the war closed. She showed me the gourd with a few grains still left.

And there were the hand gourds also on that long water shelf. A hand gourd was one of the flat round ones with a hand hole cut between neck and the main bulge. I carried water in a small one when I was a very small girl. One of the first tasks on the farm was carrying my Father water in the fields in one.

One variety grew as large or almost as large as a half bushel measure. The top sawed off served as hens nest. And around some hand looms some had string handles and served as a basket to hold the quills of thread for weaving as a quill was needed every few moments this would hang right at hand.

And last but not least they served as rattles for the baby. Take a straight handled one scrape it dry it will shake the seed loose. It was slick no splinters. no paint it was bangable it rattled just the thing for a baby sitting alone. So you see the lowly gourd played an important useful part in the life of the early settlers.

P. S. and there was the nest egg gourd which thrifty housewives planted and used as nest eggs. They were exactly the shape and size of an egg that old dommer and old top knot could be completely fooled by them. And most of the sewing baskets contained another species a little larger to slip in that blue wool sock or those heavy woolen stockings to darn on the holes.

Log Rolling

When I was a small girl, when a man cleared a piece of land the big logs of oak, pine, hickory and what not, was cut into convenient lengths. As one man couldn't possibly handle them, he could invite the strongest men in the community to what was called a log rolling. There would be six to eight men to log. They used sticks called hand sticks which were pushed under the log and with a man on either side and two men to the stick, with much puffing and grunting then would arise in unison. By keeping step they could carry the biggest logs. When reaching a heap of logs they would all let go of one accord, putting the log on the heap to be burned.

Sometimes there would be eight or ten men to a log and it would thrill me to watch them. They lived in cabins and burned millions of feet of hard lumber. Meanwhile the housewives were just as busy preparing deep chicken pie, baked ham, pumpkin and sweet potato pies. All these good things were usually prepared also for corn shuckings, cotton pickings and quiltings. Everybody had corn shuckings and sometimes the men would shuck until midnight. In some communities there used to be a jug of whiskey hidden to

118

encourage the men when their spirits began to lag or they grew sleepy. Our people were temperate so there was no whiskey needed.

There wasn't a piano in our settlement, one or two organs. There were fiddles, banjos, Jew's harps, harps and harmonicas. Strict Christian people wouldn't allow a fiddle or banjo player in their homes. I don't know why unless it made them want to dance. I don't suppose there was ever one heard in the Mitchell home. They looked on them with scorn. Lot of ignorant people as you will find out by reading as I am one step removed. No not one step.

> I had a Jew's harp some years ago when our children were young. It is a small simple musical instrument consisting of a lyre-shaped metal frame containing a metal tongue, which is plucked while the frame is held in the teeth. The vibrations causing twanging tones. The Jew's harp was known for centuries all over Europe. Found in all parts of the world under various names. No apparent reason for associating it with the Jews.

People dont exclaim then like they do at present. We say Huh! They exclaimed, Whee eeh! and Hoo ee!

Biscuit or any kind of wheat bread was called cake so the two breads went by the name of corn bread and cake. Cake was called pound cake to distinguish it from wheat bread.

When a young person went to school and caught the idea of calling things and names properly he was accused of departing from the good old ways and of trying to talk proper. He was called 'biggity', 'Stuck up' etc.

They said thar, haint, hit for it, younes, yourn, way over yonder, some said yander some younder, yam side, tother side, yaller, air for are, wush for wish, praeumonney for pneumonia, rheumatism was known as roomatiz, neuralgia was called neuralgy, a jaundice condition was yaller janders, a horse was known as a creeter by some and a crigger by others. Your waggin meant your wagon. Ask an old timer about the health of his family, wal we air jest sorter middlin at or horse, and if they were well add gaily.

Chapter 19

1936
Styles and Customs a Century ago.

When a girl I used to listen to my Aunts tell of the styles and customs when they were girls which is close to a century now. The only way to attend church was by walking or horse back. They said they usually preferred walking. They had nice slippers, I believe imported, with rubber bows. They either wore their everyday shoes or went barefooted. In sight of the church, they put on their sandals or slippers or what they were. They said a pair lasted a long time. There was no rouge, they gave their cheeks a pinching or rubbed them with the under side of a dog wood leaf. This brought the blood to their cheeks.

The bleaching the face and neck, honey or milk was used, for face powder they used corn meal, wheat flour or white clay. If they wished to black their shoes, sweet milk, molasses and soot was used. The had no hair pins, they had not been invented and did not come into general use until after I could remember.

There are still some of the old timers tying up their hair with a string. She would take one end of a string in her mouth, holding on and winding the other end of string around and around that knob of hair which stuck out like a club and sometimes like a ham. No wonder women after marrying wore caps. When I first remember caps were going out and some kind of home knit hair net was worn. Some of the up to date ones tied their hair with some kind of piece of eel skin. It would induce growth, what was wanted with more is beyond me.

The extremely stylish in colonial days cut it off and wore

a wig. Her world didn't have any cold cream, vanishing cream, rouge, finger nail polish, hair curlers, no lip stick, eyebrow pencil, hair pens or any ready made shoe strings. She tied her shoes with leather or cotton strings. Except ribbon for best slippers.

For a period of years huge hoop skirts were in style, my Aunts still had theirs, they were huge affairs worn with extremely wide petticoats and skirts. If a door was narrow it wouldn't go through without scooting out to one side. They were ridiculous.

Her remedy for chapped hands was a cake of mutton tallow.

Did you catch that, the underside of a green dogwood leaf will, when rubbed on the cheek, bring color to the cheeks.

Soap Making

Every old fashioned home when I was a child had what was known as an ash hopper. Sometimes built of scrap lumber sometimes a section of hollow tree which was set up on a platform, this receptacle was filled with ashes which had been removed from some of those 6 by 8 or 10 foot fireplaces where oak and hickory had been burned through the winter.

This in turn has water poured into a depression in the ashes and it dripped slowly to be caught at the bottom. This liquid was called lye this in turn was mixed with grease and boiled into soap. Amongst the Negro mammys (and some whites too) there was a lot of superstition the moon had to be in a certain phase there couldn't but one person stir it and that with a sassafras stick in fact it was bad luck to burn sassafras wood indoors or out but seemed to exert some magic power over the soap pot.

Well after this soap was made it was used for toilette purposes such as face hands and the men shaved with it and there was this to say in its favor if it didn't leave a skin you would love to touch it was famous for removing dirt.

Styles of Clothing

The woman wore all the way from 9 to 15 yards in one dress. Some had 18 yards. My mother and Grandmothers skirts were so voluminous. When they should be walking I'd take a run and go as it was called then, and wrap myself from head to toe and walk along with them. There was room to spare and they swept the ground to boot. All the ladies dresses were made at home, also the mens clothing, and of all the original ideas and cuts and fits. Some of them fitted nicely and were made neatly but the majority of them were not.

I have in mind one awkward, gangling young man whose kind mother carded, wove and spun her sons suits also made them. His trouser seams wouldn't go down on the outside of the leg as it should but crept around on top of his shin bone. His coat was too tight in the shoulder and waist but when it reached the bottom it flared out like nobody's business. I feel sure if you had a duplicate of that coat you could sell it to Charlie Chaplin (the actor) for a neat sum.

I had an Aunt who was a coat and 'britches maker' (so

New Shoes and White Collars - 1900's

called then) better known as a seamstress now. She did it all by hand. They fitted nicely. She would take her home spun sewing thread and pull it across a small cake of bees wax. When that thread passed through the wool cloth there was a faint musical sound. When she sewed anything she back stitched it. The seam would last as long as the garment.

I didn't see a hip pocket on mens trousers until I was grown, their britches as they called them had two pockets in front where they are to be found now. Their shirts opened and were buttoned up the back. Everyday ones had a straight band around the neck. Their best shirts were also white, had a mass of small tucks or ruffles in front and some plain but these shirts were starched until they were as stiff as a board. Never saw a shirt with color until I was grown. The old ladies would vie with each other to see who could keep the men folk shirts whitest.

There was a style of trousers dated back, farther back than I can remember, that two or three elderly gentlemen clung on to — made in front like ladies knickers are now and were buttoned on the sides. These didn't have a sign of pocket. Do you suppose that style will ever return?

Hat Maker

My father told me about a hat maker he visited when he was a little boy, to get his head measured for a hat. He said the man had sorts and sizes of wooden blocks and wooden knobs to fit these hats on, very appropriate don't you think. Wool was taken with scalding water, a wooden mallet was used to beat it into a pulp and spread over afore mentioned block. I don't imagine they measured up to the Stetson in beauty and fit.

Those wool hats had high roomy crowns and men carried what they called their possibles in the crowns. This was a handkerchief called 'Hand-ercheer' goose quill pen, if a business man, and a paper snuff box. This snuff being used in the nose. I don't suppose hat raising to the ladies was practical. My father said when he was a small boy several old men he knew carried their snuff boxes and sniffed into their noses. The water would run out of their nose and eyes and there was a lot of sneezing.   Let me introduce you to the average young man in shirt sleeves of the early 1880's. No hip pockets, a pleat or fold stitched down on the outside of his trouser legs, white shirt buttoned up in the back, a high straight band around his neck meeting at back of neck unless he had a stiff separate front to wear for best with shirt studs stuck up and down in front with a paper or celluloid collar or sometimes a linen one. The good wife had a hard time starching and ironing those accessories. I don't suppose there was a laundry in the United States. If he wore a straw hat at all in the summer it was black. I can't remember seeing any white ones.

Men wore suspenders, known as gallese, very few manufactured ones, some were knit some were several thicknesses of cloth sewn together. The cloth ones were very substantial, wouldn't give one bit when a man stooped.

Some of the kind of work Mother did was weaving jeans. It was a thick milled cloth for making men suits. It was usually died either blue or brown. Sometimes it had small flecks of white, a dark red or brown and was called mixed jeans. The blue was dyed in some kind of process with the extract of indigo. It came in cakes like chocolate. Something called madder was added. The large wash boiler had to be set in one corner of the Kitchen fireplace and kept warm for a week or two. Wheat bran was tied up in a budget and added. It almost outdid a witches caldron in mysteries, smell etc. The hanks of wool thread were added to this. I have never in all my life seen anything so blue and so beautiful a blue as the old women dyed. They dyed both cotton and wool and it was pretty as long as there was a scrap of it. Dying brown was much simpler.

My dad had a shawl. Lots of men wore either shawls or what was known as capes. It would do you good and be an unforgettable experience to have met some of the old characters. I knew who didn't know B from a bull foot, hear their opinions expressed in their own original way and how their minds work. No standardization then, no high school turning out girls and boys with the same manner of speaking etc.

Manners

No college men in the country, I mean in our community, no suave hat tipping gentlemen. They would enter our home with their bell crowned wool hats planted firmly on their heads, didn't ever know it was polite to take them off.

There were families where the children were not allowed to talk aloud at the table. Polite children were taught to say "Yes Sir" "No Sir" "Yes Ma'am" and "No Mam". Hat raising at the ladies was not practiced. Some men would come into the house and if it was cold would keep their hat on. I've wondered if men still wore boots and whiskers if they still couldn't have lorded it over his wife until now. With a thatch of whiskers concealing his expression he could keep her guessing what he was thinking about. When whiskers and boots went out of style and he shaved those whiskers off, maybe his wife could tell what he was thinking. He lost some of the blustering, cock of the walk. My belief is if the men ever want to look and act like liege lords of the creation and impress the ladies they will have to wear whiskers again. No I'm not joking, there is a grain of truth in it.

A liege lord is one entitled to allegiance and service.

Changes in Last Hundred Years in Addressing Parents

Grandfather Mitchell called his Daddy and Mammy.
His children said Pap and Mother.
We called ours Pa and Ma.
Grandmother Crain said Daddy and Mammy.
Her children addressed them as Father and Mother.
Uncle Sam Crains daughters said Pappy and
      Mammy as did many other families.
      The sons said Father and Mother.
But around Civil War time the parents were called
      Pap and Mother mostly.
So everything changes in styles — everything in
      fact except human nature and the goodness of
      the human heart!

Chapter 20

Schools, Grave Diggers

Well Marcelle, I am not making fun for I am only one step removed from them as you will find out in reading this. I have never gone to school (all told) more than 12 months. Free school ran for 2 or 3 month a year I don't know which. We had no books hardly, no grades, no equipment. We carried slates and slate pencils lots of children didn't have those. Our school was a log house with an open fireplace. There were no windows so we had to keep the door open. When say a door I mean a door as our school had only one. Our seats were backless benches with peg legs.

Our first real school house had one log, hewed out a piece and three or four window panes inserted. We had no black boards but we were well supplied with one thing. An up to date teacher usually brought in a bunch of switches and leaned them in a convenient corner never uttering a word. Some teachers would use them on the least provocation on the part of the scholars. We were all known as scholars instead of students. I had never been used to being switched at home so I had a morbid fear of those switches. He called us to books by tapping his pocket knife on the outside door facing. We played cat, bull pen and jumped ropes at recess. So what I've written will seem funny to your grandchildren if you have any and this book is preserved.

Our old Pioneers acted and talked the best they knew and so am I using my best English as I know it. You must realize we didn't have black boards, writing paper or grades. We did have slates and pencils. We had three months of school a year. Some who came to school learned to read and write and some didn't.

There were no school plays, no prizes given, no report cards. In fact no encouragement given except switches. Poor nervous teacher, he only made 25 dollars per month or at most thirty dollars. Two months in summer and one in winter. There wasn't a high school in the state. Preacher Earle had a private school at Gowensville and there was something similar at Reedville.

We had Furman University in Greenville and the Greenville Female College but poor farming people couldn't pay the price so we grew up on ignorance and I, when young, craved to go to college. As I have said I'm writing all this in bed after I'm worn out almost as to nerves and I'm growing old.

It is said that everything is thrown out in circles including the human mind so I'm nearing the end of the circle where I began. My mind is running backward instead of forward. Chewing the cud of life as it were.

Grave Digger

There was a man in the community who swore an oath every time he spoke. So one night someone came hollering and fell into Grandfather Crains door who was the same man. He told him the Devil took after him and ran him until he was exhausted. Said he could hear the chains rattling.

There was another character in the community who wore a long black beard, who had keen shifty black eyes who would shoulder his gun. It would balance there, he wouldn't touch it. He wouldn't work much leaving that for the wife and children. He had an unsavory reputation and stayed in the woods most of the time. He had hunted so much he went around with a peeking peering look and bent over a jump on you kind of look and walked with a softly stride and walked like an Indian.

This old fellow belonged to the Church part of the time. There was a rule in the church if a fellow became intoxicated he was promptly excluded without a proper acknowledgement. Well (this is no joke).

Every revival meeting this old man would come back to the Church with tears, handshaking, telling of how he had prayed over the matter, how the Good Lord had forgiven him, his whole face quivering with emotion to be received back into the full fellowship of the Church. Only sad to say, before snow flew he would go on one of his drinking sprees, running his wife and children from home, breaking dishes, cooking utensils etc. His poor old wife was the only person whom I ever saw barefoot in winter. She was a good, patient hard working old Soul with her poor old feet wrapped in strips of cloth, who never grumbled but remained true to him and her children as long as he lived. Pa said his joining the Church each summer began before I could remember.

Well his redeeming qualities were that he was a great grave digger. He could dig the straightest smoothest graves of any man around and took a pride in it as they were for the most part dug to fit the home made coffin as such a thing as a box, as a receptacle for general coffins had not come into use until after I was a good size girl and there were no flowers.

Chapter 21

Chrismas

My father made a great deal of Christmas for our sake I suppose. One Christmas stands out plainer in my memory. Christmas Day Memory:

When I was seven or eight years old what made me remember it so well it was the last time Phillip hung up his stocking at our home. Phillip was an ex-slave, he belonged to Grandfather, his Daddy, old Phillip, died a few few weeks before Phillip was born. I know how my daddy was so very kind to Phillip. On that Christmas eve night Pa let Tommie and me watch him fill his long sock. He wore number ten or eleven shoes. We put in candy, a piece of coconut, bunch raisins and other goodies, until we came to the top, next was a piece of cornbread and in the very top was a switch coiled.

Well after an eternity morning did break, we had explored the contents of our stocking, all tense waiting for Phil. All at once the silence was shattered by a loud "Christmas Gift." He had slipped up to the back door. He came in "ha ar, ha ar" that was the way he laughed. He went up to the fire place and saw where Santa Claus had scratched the back coming down. He was a good actor for us children. He stopped in open mouthed astonishment when he discovered Santa had actually put something in his sock. The very first thing he pulled out was a switch.

"Mr. Will Mr. Will what made him put in a hickory. I didn't need a whippin Mr. Will Mr. Will what made him put corn bread in I didn't want corn braid Chrismus" he kept on yum yum candy reesins coconut. In come "Miss Mary" with a cake. He was as happy as a child but he didn't hang up his sock anymore at our house.

My mother told me in after years that was his custom. He hung one sock at our house, one at "Miss Betties" at Grandmother's and Aunt Lizzies. He called Aunt Lizzie "Miss Bettie" and she saw that his sock was well filled. My daddy was kindness itself to the poor black boy. He would let him go fishing with him or if he went off from home to Greenville, etc. Phillip went along. He was a good horse boy. He stayed with (Uncle) Dr. John Mitchell and Aunt Eliza some and with us some. He had a broom in one hand and a dish rag in the other.

When I was a girl my Uncle went to Greenville found and bought something called banana. He sent my mother a piece of one for her to taste. She cut it up in buttons so we children could have a taste. She nibbled on her bit and said she liked it and said it tasted to her like musk-melon. We all liked it. We couldn't get oranges except at Christmas. I don't suppose they were shipped in any other time. We never heard of grapefruit. We didn't get any coconut except at Christmas. I don't suppose they were on the market any other time. There were plenty of apples. Wagons from North Carolina.

There was one wagon that used to pass our house. It belonged to Tinsley Ballenger and was called a Prairie schooner. I asked my Dad why the body was so tall and smooth in the back. He said it was to keep the Indians from crawling in. That was the kind wagon trains used to trek to the West in.

Greenville, SC

A tribute to Great Aunt Anah Mitchell

She was the daughter of Thomas and Mary Anne Harbin Mitchell. She was a maiden lady who lived to be 70 years old. She was very intelligent and well read and was never known to read anything trashy and cheap. I was very fond of her and it was a treat for me to be with her. She had a good memory, was well informed and well educated. She was also a devout Christian. If I have ever amounted to anything, I owe it partly to her and her influence. She read the bible daily, was devoted to her brothers and sisters, her nephews and nieces, Church and neighbors.

She was one woman who didn't indulge in gossip and if she was caught in a gossipy group would shut up like a clam. She owned a wise head and a still tongue, used good English but I failed to remember where she received her schooling but I guess she picked it up from her brothers for she had a wonderful memory and was not superstitious and she was clean minded. I counted it a great privilege to be allowed to spend the night with her. She loved to have the children to play games. When I was a little girl the three Mitchell boys would have great times in her room.

Grandfather built the present house on the east side of the road where it now stands but Aunt Anah stayed on alone in the old home which was on the lower and opposite side of the road and where she was reared. She took her meals up with the family but slept and stayed in the old home.

I enjoyed spending the night with her and and loved to hear her talk usually about books. She had read about things traditional in her family. About some white children the Indians had captured and how they were returned to their parents etc. No superstitions, no ghost stories, no obscene language. She loved us all and mothered us. She was one of the unsung heroines of which there are so many who nurse their aged parents, always on hand and ready to wait on all members of their family if needed. That was Aunt Anah.

Negress Hannah. Aunt Han I called her. Mothers cook. I don't think these memories would be complete without a word about Hannah. She had a black skin but a white soul. Mother reared her from a small girl as a cook. Han married and had 4 children all born in slavery. Her husband also a slave belonged to the Cunningham family. Mother built her a cabin. Philip, her husband, died. So after the war and she was freed she stayed until Mother died. She was a Christian and practiced all the Christian virtues. She was industrious, truthful, honest, strictly honest and virtuous. She loved her white folks and after I was married she came to see us as long as she lived.

Maybe you Ansel remember during Christmas she came and brought us one of those huge red stripped sticks of candy (you were about two and a half or three years old). So when she came in she said she bought the candy to give to the one that kissed her. She sat down so you walked and walked around her chair — she didn't let on. After a while you asked her if her feet were white so we found out you meant to kiss her if you could find a white spot. She had a keen sense of humor. She laughed and laughed so you got the candy as she brought it especially to you and was far too well bred to have allowed you to kiss her. Blessings on her memory.

More about Funerals

I meant to say those coffins were as innocent of handles as a door knob is of hair. No soft music, no flowers, and after the ghostly thing was lowered into the ground and partly filled with clay some fellow jumped into that grave and tramped and tramped like he had planted a tree. Attending Church was called guine. Goin to meetin and the Church house was known as the meetin house, I'd venture to say, by 99% of the population.

Chapter 22

Muster Days

My father used to tell us of muster days and what an event in his life when a boy especially general muster which was held I think once a year. The people for miles around attended. Of the preparations made to attend Ma owned what was known as a Dutch Oven, an outdoor affair kind of furnace and baked ginger bread in it. It baked huge pones or as you might say by the wholesale. I don't know that she baked it to sell or not. Anyway there was much roasting and baking done the day before the event and everybody who could went.

I think the general muster was held at a place known as Brutons Old Field quite near our house. There was the marching drilling, shooting rifle practice, and the hundreds of men. Well its up to you, Ansel, to imagine as you have been in the army. Anyway all the time wasn't spent drilling.

There was horse racing fist and skull fights,

Ansel gives niece Alice a whirl on return from France.

134

wrestling matches, speech making. Pa said somebody would bring kegs of brandy, some barrels of whiskey to sell. Some barrels of cider went with the ginger bread and stood for ice cream today. He said a young man would treat his best girl to a slice of that bread and a mug of apple cider.

He said in the afternoons after this there would be soldiers imbided freely these fights would start he said there would form a ring of men around. Such hollowing and cheering them. They would fight until one went under and he said he never knew of a shooting at one. If I remember the mornings were for drilling and the afternoons for fun and on election years lots of candidates and speeches etc. He said there was a platform for speakers on the grounds.

Muster in New York 1943

Furman University was a school thirteen miles from my home in Greer, South Carolina. It was a pleasant institution of learning nestled in the city of Greenville. Perhaps I should say crowded into the city. Trees shaded the area in summer. We would often take the five to ten minutes walk downtown for a break from the daily routine. This was a good time. University life seemed right for me.

A year after high school graduation I was working full time as a clerk in Robert Turner's grocery store. At this same time, a year after graduating from college, a young lady was hired to teach at Greer High School. The difference of a few years in age was a major concern for this 18 year old. I grew a mustache . . . that I remember. The details of how I was able to get a date with her are overshadowed by the date itself.

She was rooming in a house not far from the high school about three blocks from downtown. I had no car which wasn't unusual in those days. After stopping by to get her, we walked to the Grand Theater and on our way we passed several of my friends sitting on the curb between the furniture store and sidewalk. Ordinarily I would have been sitting with them watching the parade of movie goers ... this night I was in the parade.

After the movie we were sitting in the back yard of the house where she lived. We talked about her college days, her first year of teaching biology and how she liked it. She encouraged me to go to college, talked about the importance of education and how she liked teaching. I listened I think maybe in her kind way, she was telling me you are too young to be dating me. Your tomorrow will come but your education must come first.

The years passed and on the 7th day of December 1941, I was driving from our home in Greer to the farm of my Hawkins grandparents.. The trees were smaller then and from time to time I could see the southern edge of the Blue Ridge Mountains. My car radio was on and the regular program was interrupted. My first reaction was this must be another Orson Wells thriller. In a moment I pulled over to the shoulder of the road and stopped. I listened in disbelief. I wanted the message to be repeated. It was. The Japanese had bombed our fleet at Pearl Harbor and our air base on the Island of Oahu.

I continued my studies at Furman University. In the spring of 1943 I graduated with a B.S. degree in . . . no not biology, but chemistry. That spring was the end of my studies at Furman. I was waiting for orders to report for training in the navy.

A year earlier I had taken a bus trip to Charlotte, North Carolina.It was the second effort I made to join the military service. On my initial attempt I did not pass the physical for the air force. The navy came next. With them I had better luck.

After graduation I waited for orders. Early summer of '43 was spent as a life guard at Chicks Spring, a popular but very very small man made lake.

On July 15, 1943 I received my orders from the Director of Naval Officer Procurement in Atlanta, Georgia. The first paragraph was right to the point:

> *"You are ordered hereby to active duty with pay and directed to proceed and report to the Commanding Officer, U.S. Naval Reserve Midshipman School, Furnald Hall, Columbia University, New York, New York, on August 2, 1943 for approximately one month's active duty with pay as an Apprentice Seaman, Class V-7, U.S. Navel Reserve."*
> *(Note the term 'with pay' is mentioned two times in the above.)*

*I immediately shaved off my mustache. I wanted
to blend in not stand out in a bunch of raw recruits. If
I hadn't been under orders to report to Columbia University
I would have viewed New York from a different perspective.
By the way, our dormitory on the campus was our 'ship'
for the duration of training.*

*Carrying my possessions in a small bag, I left the
train and got a map of the subway system and sat down to
examine it. This was the beginning of a strange new way of
life for me.*

*Grandmother Alice was spared experiencing
World War II in which several of her grandchildren
served and returned home safely.*

I remember when there were no telephones, no daily newspaper, no rural mail routes. Our present post office being 3 or 4 miles away if we had a rural carrier it was the only post office except at Wilson's Store at Highland. And after many years we secured a rural route one that came up the Jordon road and we had a box at Jordon Crossing. In nice weather our carrier could get up from Greer by 11 o'clock and in muddy rainy weather he came around one o'clock. And if there was snow and ice sometimes it would be 2 or 3 days all with a horse and buggy.

And now we have a daily paper which is brought to our front gate in an automobile. What next?

P.S. Greenville City now boasts two daily papers, the morning paper being called the Greenville News, the afternoon paper the Evening Piedmont. And a radio station WFBC. What next? and next?

P. S. Printing in those days was done on hand presses. Printing was a trade some of it being done by roving printers. When news papers became plentiful the preachers began trouncing from their pulpits on reading newspapers and especially reading them on Sunday. And it was a matter of pride for a good old brother or sister to say he or she didn't read anything but the book (meaning the Bible which was usually referred to as the book) as a Bible and an almanac was the only thing to read.

There was no weekly magazine, no comics. If there were they hadn't reached us. Don't suppose there were any type writers, no fountain pens and I was just past the goose quill age as steel points on a wooden stock were coming into use. The business man carrying his bottle of ink with him and an age back of that ink I used homemade. No wonder business men were often aflicted with writers cramp.

I used to listen in on some stiff arguments on whether the world was round or flat. Our soil contains the soil of many and old fellow who died knowing the world be resurrected from good old flat earth. He argued thusly. If the thing turned over the water would all fall out of oceans, rivers etc. and didn't the Bible say Joshua command the sun stand still and usually silence his antagonist on that.

And when my Father was a small boy he said when men came to visit and spend the night they would discuss witching and believing it. He said he was scared to death of a witch, afraid he would get a spell cast on him. The belief in witches died hard but by the time I was old enough to take notice none of our families believed in them.

And we mustnt forget ghosts. The same crowd who believed in witches believed in ghosts too. Some of them seeing some fearful sights. Ghosts have been laid low along side the witches. As you take notice I say men as the poor pioneer women without any freedom from drudgery and very few who could read. I don't believe many of them would tred there and most of them were seen and not heard. It was left to her liege Lord to form and express public opinions and his word was law.

My mother taught me and I believed her that there was no ghosts, no witches sign in dreaming, no invisible laws to transgress there was only right and wrong living as taught by the Bible. There were no invisible gods to obey to keep from having bad luck, only Jehovah God. I had school mates who were positively burdened with superstitions and I would horrify them by transgressing them.

The Mitchell family were altogether free of superstitions so my mother being Mary Ann Mitchell before marriage was free from all such trash as she alluded to it. Her law was the law of cause and effect.

May 28, 1936
Unsolved Crimes in the 'Dark Corner'

But this actually happened since I can remember.

There was an old gentleman and wife who were childless, Mr. and Mrs Milton Ponder. He died before I can remember but she and a maiden sister Nellie Page lived alone. They had grown feeble and had a nephew Milton Harrison and his wife Lou Peace Harrison move in the house with them. They had their life savings of gold and silver in blue wool sock or socks. Well one night someone knocked on their door. Milton Harrison went out and as he opened it someone threw a cloth over his head, tussled him up in a bed sheet and robbed the house of the socks of gold and silver. And the poor old ladies never recovered it and the mystery was never solved.

In the year of 1890, 1892 or perhaps 1893, there was a family of Hensleys by name who lived near Glassy Rock on Glassy Mountain. There was the mother, an elderly woman, her son Esau about 30 years old, two daughters, prospective mothers and a grandson, Willie Hensley, 12 years old. They were murdered one night, nothing was left except a few bones. What was said to have been Esau, was near the door with an axe. It seemed he might have been trying to defend them. This murder was supposed to have been committed by 5 or 6 well known young Bullies of the mountains. They are all dead now except one. They were bad Characters. There were no G Men so the murder was never solved.

Big Ben Ross was shot and killed one night, I believe in his bed. That crime was unsolved.

John L. Odom had some one take a shot at him poking the gun barrel through a knot hole. His thrifty wife had such a large fluffy feather bed, he was so deep in its downy bosoms it saved his life. He only received a bad scare and a few stray shot, mystery unsolved. He had been to Greenville and reported some distillery, Revenuer had cut it up.

Grandmother Alice had her hands overflowing taking care of the children, cooking and housework. Who helped her? Essie Greer. We called her 'Aunt Essie'. She had her bedroom upstairs and was busy from morning till night. She helped shape the lives of the children along with her many other duties.

Ernestine, John L., Helen and Mother Alice ready for a Sunday buggy ride. The three olders boys were away at college.

Chapter 23

Railroad Trains

I forgot to tell you about the railroad trains. In 1880 my Father moved ten miles below Greenville a mile east of Piedmont Cotton Mill so we lived less than a mile east of the Depot. The engines were small looked to be mostly smokestack they burned plain pine cord wood. You will always see pictures of the wood burning locomotives and some in museums but you won't see the immense stacks of wood (I mean wood yards) on the side of the road bed for the convenience of the fireman and engineer.

When fuel ran low that train would come to a grinding rattling stop. Sometimes some of the men passengers would get out and execise while they refueled with this cord wood (it would look comical today). These stops had to be made frequently and these wood fires didn't make any noise the 3 or 4 boxes or coaches made enough to make up. I was ten years old when the change on the Greenville and Columbia road was made to coal from wood.

Early one morning the farmers around and my Father included, had gone to the fields for their days work. It happened to be a damp morning when the sound carry well when all at once the air was smote with a heavy dull roaring sound in the North, in the direction of Greenville grew louder and kept coming. On it came louder and louder. There was more praying done.

The Negros began to gather in groups scared almost to death. They pronounced it the judgement day. The whites were aIarmed too. The natives called it the world coming to an end. Work was suspended as it came nearer and nearer. Someone went to the Depot to investigate and found that they had changed from wood to what was then called stone coal to distinguish from charcoal. So the rattle trap train rattled and roared its was from Greenville to Columbia.

P. S. Passengers were allowed to ride on in freight cars. I have seen them in empty boxes sitting in kitchen chairs. It was cheaper fare. I was at the depot one day to or from school and was watching a stylishly dressed couple whom I knew sitting in those chairs and when the train started it almost unseated the lady and gave her head a jerk. Our school was beyond the Depot from home so I saw all the work around the depot or rather we did a group of school fellows. One day a circus stalled on their way from Columbia to Greenville. We children ran up and down that track. Why the hands put one cage up courtesy so we couldn't have an altogether free show.

All trains were stopped on the Sabbath day.

P.S. I forgot to say that if a person had a growth or anything the doctor could get at on the outside he would secure the services of the strongest men and women and the patient was held by brute strength. I don't believe there was a drop of iodine in the world. What was the use germs had not been dreamed of. When blood poisoning set in he was said to have died of inflection.

Things We Didn't Have

I don't believe there was a barber shop, no ice unless some enterprising soul had some in a deep pit in saw dust, no ice cream, no soft bottled drinks, no bananas. There were no Christmas cards, very few ready made clothes for men, none for women, very few buggies, very few carriages. There were lots of spinning wheels and looms, lots of saddles, no lanterns, carried torches instead, no paved streets not in Greenville.

142

Taylors and Greer were not on the map,

The people I've been writing about were, on the whole God fearing people, hard working, hard fisted, sons of toil, honest too in their dealings. They hated mean things and were the salt of the earth. They built the foundation for the present so called civilization to rest on. I have sweet memories of most of them. Only their influence lives. Peace to their ashes.

Kerosene Lamp

Reese returning from Grandfathers on the road he named *Ridge*.

Mrs. Reese
(Margaret) Hawkins

DOC AND HIS KINFOLK WHO LOVED TO VISIT HIM AT THE OLD HOME PLACE.
**Right: Brian Gaskill
(painting by Lillian Hawkins)**

Cody (Doc) Hawkins   Jean Lybrand (daughter of John L.)   Allan Hawkins III

Chapter 24

My Beloved Country

I can conscientiously sing My Country Tis of Thee. I have never even in thought been untrue to my Country. Three of my Great Grandfather's land joined and I've always thought ours the greatest place in the world. I won't live to see it, Marcelle but I hope and believe you will and I'm going to venture a prophesy that in less than fifty years, South Carolina will be one vast vegetable and dairying center. A garden supplying vegetables, owing to the iodine and other mineral contents which has only been discovered in recent years, to Northern states and perhaps abroad, also condensed milk, cheese, etc.

The western sneer at our poor soil, our terraces and bags of fertilizer but we think the worms will turn. Our pure, soft drinking water, clay soil, our rivers, creeks, springs, beautiful forests and our soil here in the Piedmont region will grow anything from upland rice to rye. I firmly believe we are on the verge of a new era and South Carolina will stand second to none. If I had had a choice before being born or where I should be sent, I would have piped up and said, " Send me to dear Old Dixie". What part of Dixie? "Exactly where I am". I'm satisfied with my country provincial-minded to Nth degree. Yes and not ashamed of it.

Some of my Favorite Scripture Verses

"For God so loved the world that he gave his
only begotten son that who-so-ever believeth
on him shall not perish but have every lasting life."

"Let not your heart be troubled, ye believe
in God believe also in me."

"For I am not ashamed of the gospel for it is the
power of God unto salvation to everyone
that believeth".

103 Psalm
14th Chapter of St. John

Things I love in the Country

I love the smells of a cotton field of a dewy morning in September. I love the hazy smokey days in October with all nature clothed in riot of colors. It is my choice month of the year. It is tinged with sadness as the leaves begin to fall and is typical of the end of human life, but here is to lovely Indian summer.

I love the summer showers, the odor of old mother earth when the rain spatters the dust. At night I love to watch lightening flashes in the distance after the passing of a thunder cloud.

I love the call of the bob white and the whippoorwills song at twilight in June.

I love to gaze into the sky at the myriad of stars and wonder and wonder at the handiwork of God. It gives one the feeling that God is in his heaven and all is right in the world. Why worry about petty things.

I love to awake of a spring morning to a concert of

singing birds.

I love to retire on a cold cold windy night after a visit to the barn yard and cow stables, hear them crunching on their feed all snug and warm. A visit to the hog pens where the hogs are bedded down warm with even the dog provided for. So come snow, come sleet—I'm happy in the knowledge that all the living creatures in our care are comfortable. You can readily see I am a farmer at heart.

I love a beautiful soft clinging snow that transforms every brown and naked twig, woods, fences, buildings, etc. to a fairyland. Read, Snow-Bound by John Greenleaf Whittier. I think it is one of the most beautiful poems I know.

I love beautiful sunsets with all the beautiful changing indescribable gorgeous colorings and am lost in wonder at each one viewed.

I love to gaze on the mountain ranges that hardly ever look alike. Its ever changing beauty outdoes any planting by man.

I love the beautiful fragrant flowers both wild and cultivated. I think God speaks to us through nature. I can see him in flowers, trees, beautiful sunsets, in the big tumbled, jumbled thunder heads, and in the soft summer breezes.

What is more restful than to sit on the bank of a clear branch or brook and hear the water gurgle, splash and sometimes almost laugh its way to the sea and how the fish and other creatures have such a happy home. You know it is home to them.

I love the last red rays of a winter sunset falling on a distant pine forest.

I love the miracle of young growing things, young crops, young buds as they slowly unfold into leaves and young animals—not to say anything of children.

I think God could have created a more interesting world if he had wished but I don't think he did. The changing seasons, all the beautiful mysteries is old but ever new to me and something I never grow tired of and let me whisper you a secret, I hate to die and leave it all.

I love loyalty to God, loyalty to God. Loyalty to ones

146

parents, loyalty to ones husband if one has a husband. Loyalty to ones friends, to ones children, ones church and ones country, including all the other things one should be loyal to.

Things I hate
Lying—
   either white or black lies
Unthankfulness
Back-biting

Sabbath breaking
Sin in all forms
Evil thoughts
Drunkness

Dear Son,
   Please let no one see this as it is badly done. I only set all this down so you might sometime draw from it. It will be one link in the chain. On the other hand after you have grown old set it down for future generations.

Alice Crain Hawkins - 66 years
February 23, 1871 - June 5, 1937

John Landrum Hawkins - 89 years
August 15, 1870 -February 8, 1960

After Ansel's death his wife Marion gave me the original memiors Grandmother Alice wrote for him. As her oldest grandson I am privileged to have a part in 'setting her stories down' for her decendants and others who cherish the history of their families who became a part of history when they arrived in America.

Grandmother Alice tells of the many inventions and changes in her lifetime constantly wondering *what next? what next?* She lived long enough to see a picture I took of the Streamliner on its 1934 maiden voyage across the country. It was considered a high tech marvel and became a leader in luxury travel. *What next?*

REESE'S

SCRAPBOOK

**Alice and John Hawkins
ready to leave for church.**

148

Author Reese's first job — driving grocery truck.
Passengers are Alice, Azalee and Connie.

1951 — Allan and his sister Meredith at a picnic at Grandmother Alice's — has the box changed since the tea party on
the back cover?

Copy of a page from the original 'book' Grandmother Alice wrote for her son, Ansel.

Story Begins Here

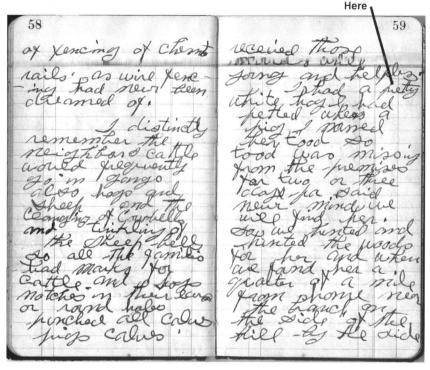

Page 60 goes on to read:

of a large log tood had banked up leaves and had found eleven little pigs and had placed them in that bed. I was almost beside myself with joy.

I had my pets. I had a pet kitten I carried around in my arms wrapped it up like a baby and that cat slept and purred in my lap nights until bedtime. I knit it booties and wrapped in blankets. We had a pet dog when on the outside named Watch wherever my brother and I went Watch went with us, and we both loved Watch. My parents didn't seem to mind us playing with them as there was no germs then.

But the sweetest and most harmless pets we had were lambs they did not last long - they soon turned into sheep and went off with the flock.

Jake and my Aunt Connie Morgan host reception for author Louis L'Amour at the Hawkins homeplace in 1975. He was researching the Carolinas for a future book.

Dr. Murphree Donnan (Ernestine's husband) longtime president of North Greenville College meets and talks with Louis.

Middle: L'Amour autographs several books for Azalee Hawkins Cook.

Bottom: Mrs. Kathy L'Amour catching up with Meredith Hawkins Wallin for a stroll along path in side yard.

Alice and Donna Hinds with their
grandmother, Ernestine H. Donnan.

**Middle: Helen's
Polly Mason.**

**Right: Allan
Hawkins and
his baby sister,
Connie Morgan.**

Meredith, Marion (Ansel's wife), Pauline (Cody's wife) examine one of Jake Morgan's antiques. He looks on from a
distance.

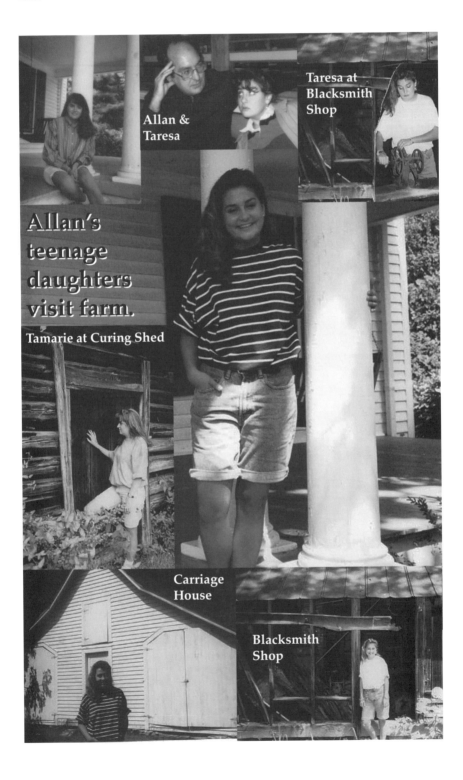

Allan &
Taresa

Taresa at
Blacksmith
Shop

Allan's teenage daughters visit farm.

Tamarie at Curing Shed

Carriage
House

Blacksmith
Shop

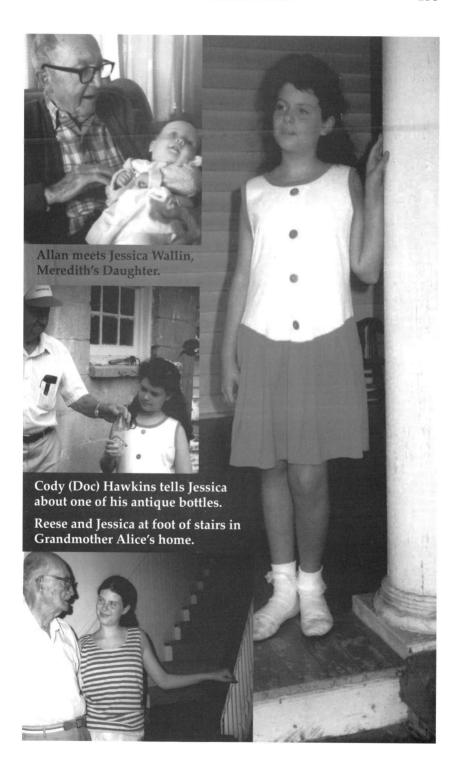

Allan meets Jessica Wallin, Meredith's Daughter.

Cody (Doc) Hawkins tells Jessica about one of his antique bottles.

Reese and Jessica at foot of stairs in Grandmother Alice's home.

154

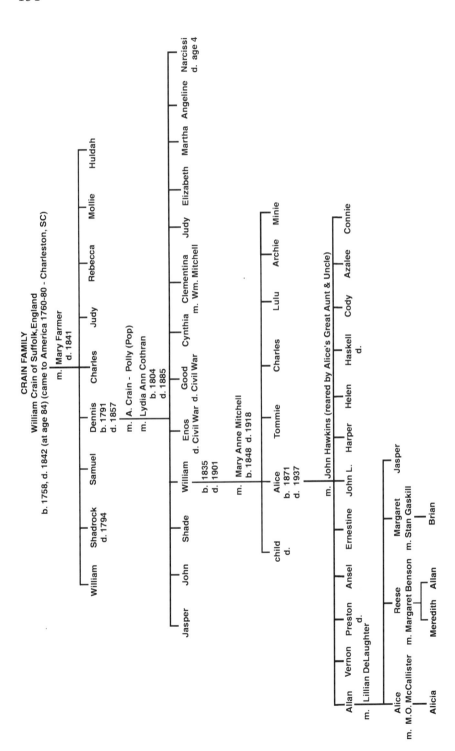

CRAIN FAMILY
William Crain of Suffolk, England
b. 1758, d. 1842 (at age 84) (came to America 1760-80 - Charleston, SC)
m. Mary Farmer
d. 1841

William

Shadrock
d. 1794

Samuel

Dennis
b. 1791
d. 1857

m. A. Crain - Polly (Pop)
m. Lydia Ann Cothran
b. 1804
d. 1885

Charles

Judy

Rebecca

Mollie

Huldah

Jasper

John

Shade

William
b. 1835
d. 1901

m. Mary Anne Mitchell
b. 1848 d. 1918

Enos
d. Civil War d. Civil War

Good

Cynthia

Clementina
m. Wm. Mitchell

Judy

Elizabeth

Martha

Angeline

Narcissi
d. age 4

child
d.

Alice
b. 1871
d. 1937

Tommie

Charles

Lulu

Archie

Minie

m. John Hawkins (reared by Alice's Great Aunt & Uncle)

Allan
m. Lillian DeLaughter

Vernon

Preston
d.

Ansel

Ernestine

John L.

Harper

Helen

Haskell
d.

Cody

Azalee

Connie

Alice
m. M.O. McCallister

Reese
m. Margaret Benson

Margaret
m. Stan Gaskill

Jasper

Alicia

Meredith

Allan

Brian

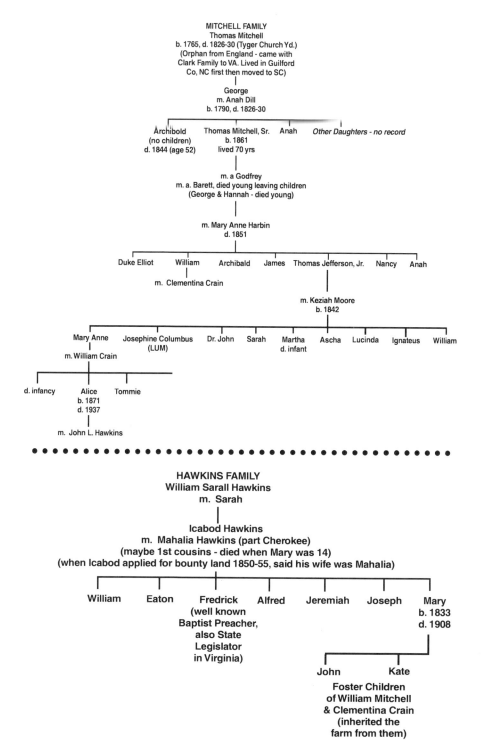

MITCHELL FAMILY
Thomas Mitchell
b. 1765, d. 1826-30 (Tyger Church Yd.)
(Orphan from England - came with
Clark Family to VA. Lived in Guilford
Co, NC first then moved to SC)

George
m. Anah Dill
b. 1790, d. 1826-30

Archibold   Thomas Mitchell, Sr.   Anah   *Other Daughters - no record*
(no children)   b. 1861
d. 1844 (age 52)   lived 70 yrs

m. a Godfrey
m. a. Barett, died young leaving children
(George & Hannah - died young)

m. Mary Anne Harbin
d. 1851

Duke Elliot   William   Archibald   James   Thomas Jefferson, Jr.   Nancy   Anah

m. Clementina Crain

m. Keziah Moore
b. 1842

Mary Anne   Josephine Columbus   Dr. John   Sarah   Martha   Ascha   Lucinda   Ignateus   William
(LUM)   d. infant

m. William Crain

d. infancy   Alice   Tommie
b. 1871
d. 1937

m. John L. Hawkins

● ●

HAWKINS FAMILY
William Sarall Hawkins
m. Sarah

Icabod Hawkins
m. Mahalia Hawkins (part Cherokee)
(maybe 1st cousins - died when Mary was 14)
(when Icabod applied for bounty land 1850-55, said his wife was Mahalia)

William   Eaton   Fredrick   Alfred   Jeremiah   Joseph   Mary
(well known   b. 1833
Baptist Preacher,   d. 1908
also State
Legislator
in Virginia)

John   Kate

Foster Children
of William Mitchell
& Clementina Crain
(inherited the
farm from them)

156

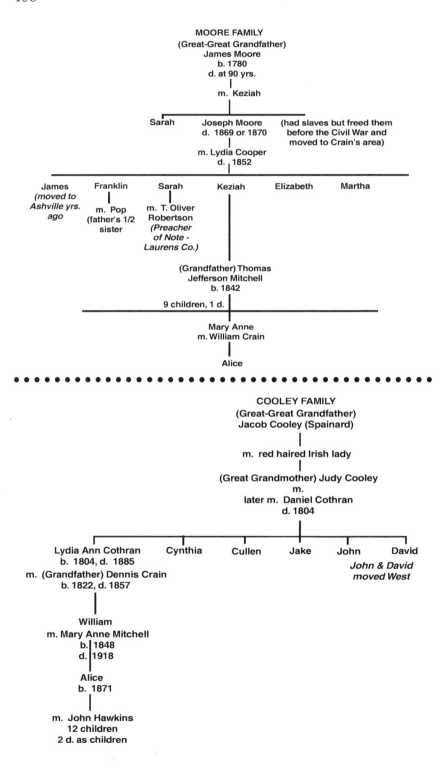

MOORE FAMILY
(Great-Great Grandfather)
James Moore
b. 1780
d. at 90 yrs.

m. Keziah

Sarah   Joseph Moore   (had slaves but freed them
d. 1869 or 1870   before the Civil War and
moved to Crain's area)

m. Lydia Cooper
d. 1852

James   Franklin   Sarah   Keziah   Elizabeth   Martha
(moved to
Ashville yrs.   m. Pop   m. T. Oliver
ago   (father's 1/2   Robertson
sister   *(Preacher*
of Note -
Laurens Co.)

(Grandfather) Thomas
Jefferson Mitchell
b. 1842

9 children, 1 d.

Mary Anne
m. William Crain

Alice

● ●

COOLEY FAMILY
(Great-Great Grandfather)
Jacob Cooley (Spainard)

m. red haired Irish lady

(Great Grandmother) Judy Cooley
m.
later m. Daniel Cothran
d. 1804

Lydia Ann Cothran   Cynthia   Cullen   Jake   John   David
b. 1804, d. 1885
m. (Grandfather) Dennis Crain   *John & David*
b. 1822, d. 1857   *moved West*

William
m. Mary Anne Mitchell
b. 1848
d. 1918

Alice
b. 1871

m. John Hawkins
12 children
2 d. as children

Camp Perry Feb, 10 # 1863

Dear Brothr and Sister hit is thrve tho kind hand of god that

I am
spared this morning to write you a few lines and the same leaves us all
well. Hopin that these few lines may soon come to hand and fine you
bouth well. I hant everything that will interest you to right. Everything
hear is stil nothing new more than common tho hant note talk of a fite
here now I haup that wont be everywhile we stay hear for
I go in a fight for them but if we do have to fite I will do best I can
for them. The health of the company is very good at this time. We
hant got but one man on the sick list now. and other companyes is
about the same amount. No bad cases on hand. We have some cold
weather hear as I ever saw everywhar. I think it has been colda nuff to
snow and rain and sleet if you call that cold wether and hit rains not
everday and we have a heep of garde duty to DO and hit is very hard
on us but takes 14 Every 24 hours that out of our compnay and
throws us on garde every three Days Besides another Duty we have
to do so a poor soldier has a hard time in camp. A man dont know
everything aBout hit unless he had tried hit. William you have hard
time you think and John have any you do in the farm is play to this
when a man is well. Dont blame no man for stain at home. I had but
one mess of meat in 4 days and sometimes not enuf bread and you
now by this we seen hard times and I am almost redied to run away
aiming hit will turn out alright sometimes all things work together for
good to them that believes in Him. My prays is for this war to come
to a close but looks to me like hit would Be obliged to come to a close
GOOD. Grant that hit may come soon. When all will return home to
Long absent friends whar we could meet at old Pleasant Hill where we
could sing our songs and prays together well mentally. William I will tell
you a Bout our meetings here for four weaks everyDay and Knight
that hit was not a rain. Mr. Vaughn come down and preached for us
and the boys seemed to be interested in the Meeting and we have a

good meeting tho it was a rain. and tho was prodestant hear. A
Sunday they was a lot of men standing around the women side and
only two thar looked very strong to see. To meney men and no
wimen the meeing seemed to do a heep of good. So I will Bring my
letter to a close I hain roat Everything that will interest you for I cant rite
Like I want to I cant rights you cant spell I want you to rite to us soon. I
remain your loven Brother until death.

Enos

158

R.G. SMITH, 11
EDITOR-IN-CHIEF

T. W. CROXTON ,'11
BUSINESS MANAGER

A. R. HAWKINS, '12
ASST. BUSINESS MANAGER

THE RICHMOND COLLEGE MESSENGER

Approved by the Retail Merchants Association of Richmond

RICHMOND, VA., December 15. 1910

Dear Mother:

I guess you think there is something wrong since you have not heard from us for some time. We have both actually been too busy to write. Examinations are almost on us and you know what that means.

We got our suits O.K. We also had to get some shirts, ties etc. Following is a statement of money paid out.

2 Suits including shirts, pant, ties etc.	$44.00
Laundry and washing	2.00
Two months board	22.00
	$ 68.00

Leaving in the bank $6.00 with which I wish to pay our Society dues. Following is what we are due College:

A. R. H. fees due	$26.00
W.V.H. " "	$38.50
Total due	$64.50

When will Pa be able to send rest of money?

Do as you think best about the box, Maybe it will be too much trouble. We get something to eat up during Christmas anyway.

I won out on my debate, and shall, if nothing happens, represent our society in a public debate to be held here 2nd Friday night in January. That means a whole lot of work for me during holidays.

Pardon such a broken letter for I have not time to write any more. Will write a long letter when we get through with exams.

Merry Christmas to all

Your loving Son,

A.R.Hawkins

June 4, 1912

"I made my degree all O.K. The list has been posted. Am to send you all an invitation. According to your letter I will not expect Pa. I realize something about what he has to do. Guess I shall get home Friday week."

A.R.H.

Richmond College
Sunday Night
Jan. 29,1911

Dear Mother,
 I shall try to pay our just debt by answering your appreciated letter. This leaves us both well. Hope you are all able to navigate. I am a little tired right now, however, as I went to Sunday School this morning and to the theater this afternoon. But you say, "What? Going to the theatre on Sunday?" Peace be still. Let me explain my position and assuage your impending wrath. This was not a regular matinee burt a lecture given by Wendell one of the greatest speakers in the U. S. He spoke here in the academy of music, the classiest theater in Richmond. His theme was Jesus of Nazareth. There was no admission fee. It was a spiritual, Rhetorical and intellectual feast.

Richmond, Virginia
October 6, 1912

Dear Mother,
 It was yesterday I received your kind letter. I am always glad to hear from home. Along with the little doings about home comes to me a vision of South Carolina. -- its cotton fields mountains and friends. Those little things which seem trivial within themselves are interesting to me because they come from home.
 I suppose you are all busy down there gathering the crops. I am equally busy though in a different way. I certainly have enough work to keep me busy all day and part of the night. I am finding my classes a great deal more interesting this year. But somewhat harder.
 We organized our soph. class the other day. I tried to get the fellows not to run me. Tip Sanders was elected. We tied. He won by one the second ballot. I feel good over the results as I had not gotten acquainted with all the fellows. I carried the Co-eds pretty solid, I think.
 I paid my board bill. We are getting very good board at the Refectory. I learned the place where A.R. boarded has come back to $11.00 a mo. I aim to go up there with one of the boys and if it is good I'll move up there to cut expenses.
 Kiss Cody for me (better wash his face first I guess, tell him). I hope Aunt Kate is well. Tell A.R. not to exceed the speed limit picking cotton. Tell all the boys to be smart like I am when I 'm at home.

Write every week,
your loving son, Vernon

 I must make some arrangements for having my shoes mended and ought to get a pr. of rubbers for walking to meals in the rain and slush (rubbers can wait but I need the half soles to save my shoes). That is all I think of now. I close with wishing you and all those you love one wish that your lives may be woven a golden thread, as happy, as beautiful, and as good as the litte gods of joy can bring.

Philologian Literary Society

RICHMOND COLLEGE

RICHMOND, VA.

Dec.3o,1911.

Dear Mother:-

I received your registered letter a few days ago and I
should have answered it earlier but have kept putting it off.
Well, I hope you all had a fine Christmas. I have had a very good
one myself. Everything has been very quiet. For the most of the
time I have been the only one in my building. I guess W.V. told
you that he sent me $7.50 to take a trip to Washington But I
was afraid to risk myself on that amount from here to Washington
and back. And when I got my suit I was almost obliged to get
some collars,socks,ties,etc. So I decided that I had rather use
the money that way than to take chances in Washington. I appreciate
the money all the same. I have spent very little money this
Christmas foolishly and still have had a very fine time. The
lady with whom I am boarding treated me very well indeed. We
had turkey etc. several time. She also gave me a small box of
fruits and nuts which xx was very acceptable. I worked Friday
and Saturday before Christmas for the same man that W.V. worked
for last year. I guess W.V will be back at school before you
get this so I shall write him there. I expect that I will have
to have some help about getting books for the Winter Term.
Write soon. With best wishes to all,

lovingly,

Allan H

WAR WORK COUNCIL

ARMY AND NAVY
YOUNG MEN'S CHRISTIAN ASSOCIATION

September 15, 1917
Wed. 4:30 P.M.

Dear Mother,

I received your letter today and am always glad to get the news from the mountains. We have just taken our third and I think last dose para-typhoid, so I am taking advantage of the rest to write letters, In case we go to France we will be inoculated for French Fever. The regulars have already taken it so I imagine they will be moved shortly. I have about concluded that we will be here some time yet.

Our new 1st LT. has just returned from France where he drove an ambulance. He related some of his experiences. He has the point of a projectile which killed two men riding in a wagon. The shell exploded while he was passing. The shock knocked him unconscious. He says the Germans will shoot at an ambulance just as quick as the enemy. It is somewhat serious to hear someone who knows the facts.

I am glad Ernestine can go to school again. Tell Harper he had better be glad he is free.

We have a new Victrola and piano at the YMCA. The U.S. spends a lot to entertain her boys but in spite of it all they get lonesome sometimes.

Have you plenty of fried chicken now? I would like to have one or two fried properly with some biscuit, but I haven't seen a biscuit since the 20th of July except a raw one. One of the boys was eating one which he got from home.

But do not dare to send such if you have as much to do as usual because I am living alright. We have not been paid one cent since we have been in service but I think surely they will pay us sometime this week. My arm is getting right sore by now so I will close for this time.

Tell all the Kiddies Hello. Yours Devotedly,

Ansel

Letters service men wrote home while stationed on our destroyer during World War II were written on V-Mail. Each letter was censored. You will note circle in the top left hand section. Under is found "CENSOR STAMP'. The letter form was more or less regular letter size and was reduced prior to leaving postal service (in this case San Francisco). This procedure reduced the load of mail which was sent by air.

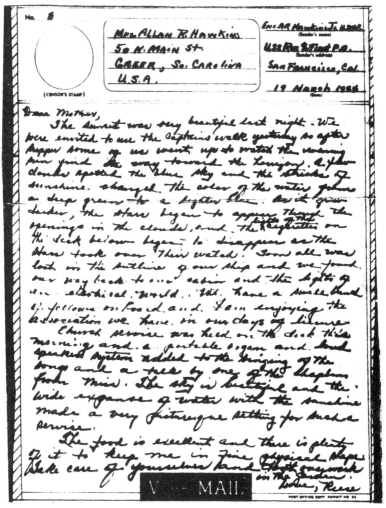

The above is a copy (slightly enlarged) of a letter sent by Ensign Reese Hawkins to his mother at Greer, SC on 19 March 1944 enroute aboard a troop transport to his assigned destroyer in the South Pacific.

Photo courtesy of john m. steiner - Jamestown Sun, Jamestown, ND

ABOUT THE AUTHOR

Reese Hawkins is a native of Greer, South Carolina. He received an Associate of Arts from North Greenville College at Tigerville and continued his education at Furman University, Greenville, South Carolina where he received a B.S. degree in Chemistry.

After service in World War II, he earned a B.S. degree in Pharmacy at North Dakota State University in Fargo. For many years Hawkins was pharmacist-owner of drug stores in Gulford College, North Carolina and Jamestown, North Dakota.

After selling his Jamestown store in 1977 he spent twenty years as a neighbor of his uncle, Cody (Doc) Hawkins, in the Pleasant Hill section of Greenville County and in Greer, South Carolina. He and his wife, Margaret, a North Dakotan from Bottineau, moved back to Jamestown in 1998 where he has an office in Meidinger Square. It was here with the help of his daughter, Meredith Wallin, he finished his first book, *Remembering Louis L'Amour.*

In the same location his second book, *Grandmother Alice* was completed.

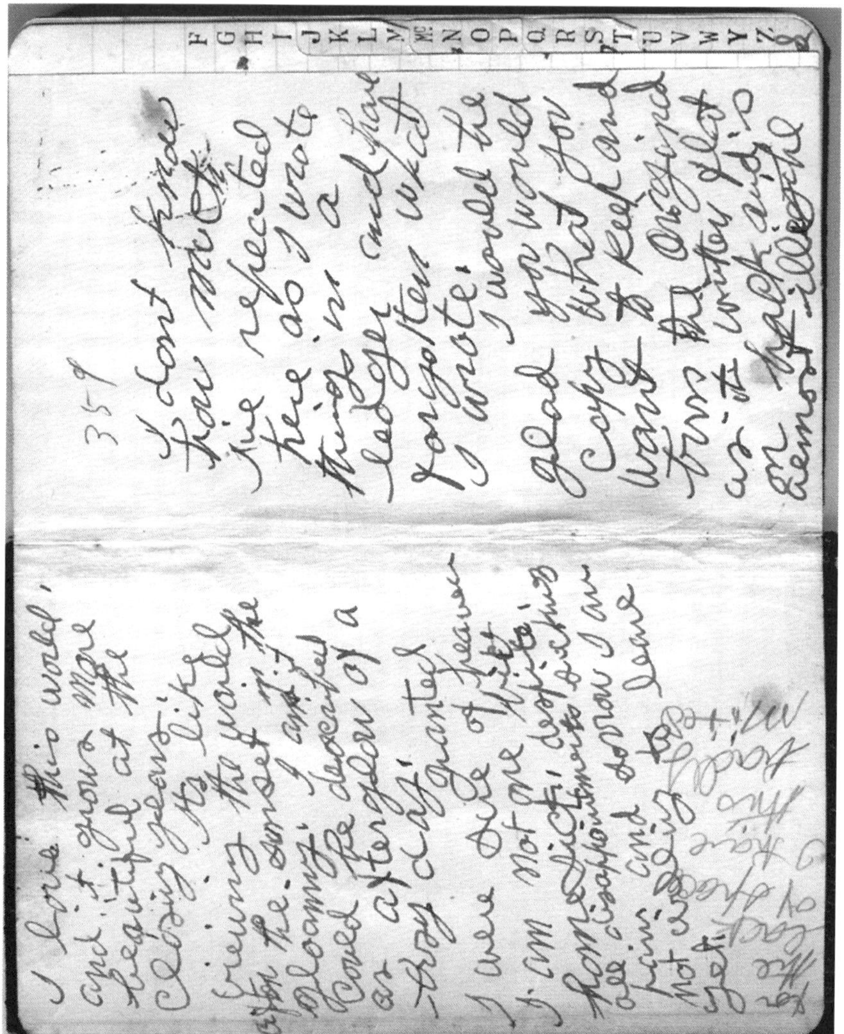

359

I dont know
how much
I've expected
thee so I wrote
things in a
ledger and have
forgotten what
I wrote. I would be
glad you would
copy what you
want to keep and
from the Original
from it written plat
as it written plat and
remove illegible

I love this world,
and it grows more
beautiful at the
closing years.
.. seeing the world
.. at the sunset of the
.. blooming, I am
Covered, decorated of a
.. an afterglow of a
.. cay granted
I were sure of heaven.
I am not one who
.. Romantic dreaming sketches
.. and sorrow I am
.. not working ..

❏ **Check here to order additional copies of**
GRANDMOTHER ALICE

❏ **Check here to order additional copies of**
REMEMBERING LOUIS L'AMOUR

$16.95 EACH
(plus $3.95 shipping & handling for first book,
add $2.00 for each additional book ordered.

Shipping and Handling costs for larger quantites
available upon request.

Please send me _____ GRANDMOTHER ALICE
_____ REMEMBERING LOUIS L'AMOUR additional books at
$16.95 + shipping & handling

Bill my: ❏ VISA ❏ MasterCard Expires _____

Card # _____

Signature _____

Daytime Phone Number _____

For credit card orders call 1-888-568-6329
TO ORDER ON-LINE VISIT: www.jmcompanies.com
OR SEND THIS ORDER FORM TO:
McCleery & Sons Publishing
PO Box 248
Gwinner, ND 58040-0248

I am enclosing $_____ ❏ Check ❏ Money Order
Payable in US funds. No cash accepted.

SHIP TO:

Name_____

Mailing Address _____

City _____

State/Zip _____

Orders by check allow longer delivery time.
Money order and credit card orders will be shipped within 48 hours.
This offer is subject to change without notice.

NEW RELEASES

I Took The Easy Way Out
Life Lessons on Hidden Handicaps
Twenty-five years ago, Tom Day was managing a growing business - holding his own on the golf course and tennis court. He was living in the fast lane. For the past 25 years, Tom has spent his days in a wheelchair with a spinal cord injury. Attendants serve his every need. What happened to Tom? We get an honest account of the choices Tom made in his life. It's a courageous story of reckoning, redemption and peace. Written by Thomas J. Day. (200 pgs.)
$19.95 each in a 6x9" paperback.

Tales & Memories of Western North Dakota
Prairie Tales & True Stories of 20th Century Rural Life
This manuscript has been inspired with Steve's antidotes, bits of wisdom and jokes (sometimes ethnic, to reflect the melting pot that was and is North Dakota; and from most unknown sources). A story about how to live life with humor, courage and grace along with personal hardships, tragedies and triumphs.
Written by Steve Taylor. (174 pgs.)
$14.95 each in a 6x9" paperback.

9/11 and Meditation
America's Handbook
All Americans have been deeply affected by the terrorist events of and following 9-11-01 in our country. David Thorson submits that meditation is a potentially powerful intervention to ameliorate the frightening effects of such divisive and devastating acts of terror. This book features a lifetime of harrowing life events amidst intense pychological and social polarization, calamity and chaos; overcome in part by practicing the age-old art of meditation.
Written by David Thorson. (110 pgs.)
$9.95 each in a 4‑1/8 x 7-1/4" paperback.

Phil Lempert's HEALTHY, WEALTHY, & WISE
The Shoppers Guide for Today's Supermarket
This is the must-have tool for getting the most for your money in every aisle. With this valuable advice you will never see (or shop) the supermarket the same way again. You will learn how to: save at least $1,000 a year on your groceries, guarantee satisfaction on every shopping trip, get the most out of coupons or rebates, avoid marketing gimmicks, create the ultimate shopping list, read and understand the new food labels, choose the best supermarkets for you and your family. Written by Phil Lempert. (198 pgs.)
$9.95 each in a 6x9" paperback.

Miracles of COURAGE
The Larry W. Marsh Story
This story is for anyone looking for simple formulas for overcoming insurmountable obstacles. At age 18, Larry lost both legs in a traffic accident and learned to walk again on untested prothesis. No obstacle was too big for him - putting himself through college - to teaching a group of children that frustrated the whole educational system - to developing a nationally recognized educational program to help these children succeed. Written by Linda Marsh. (134 pgs.)
$12.95 each in a 6x9" paperback.

The Garlic Cure

Learn about natural breakthroughs to outwit: Allergies, Arthritis, Cancer, Candida Albicans, Colds, Flu and Sore Throat, Environmental and Body Toxins, Fatigue, High Cholesterol, High Blood Pressure and Homocysteine and Sinus Headaches. The most comprehensive, factual and brightly written health book on garlic of all times. INCLUDES: 139 GOURMET GARLIC RECIPES!

Written by James F. Scheer, Lynn Allison and Charlie Fox. (240 pgs.)
$14.95 each in a 6x9" paperback.

For Your Love

Janelle, a spoiled socialite, has beauty and breeding to attract any mate she desires. She falls for Jared, an accomplished man who has had many lovers, but no real love. Their hesitant romance follows Jared and Janelle across the ocean to exciting and wild locations. Join in a romance and adventure set in the mid-1800's in America's grand and proud Southland.

Written by Gunta Stegura. (358 pgs.)
$16.95 each in a 6x9" paperback.

From Graystone to Tombstone

Memories of My Father Engolf Snortland 1908-1976
This haunting memoir will keep you riveted with true accounts of a brutal penitentiary to a manhunt in the unlikely little town of Tolna, North Dakota. At the same time the reader will emerge from the book with a towering respect for the author, a man who endured pain, grief and needless guilt -- but who learned the art of forgiving and writes in the spirit of hope.

Written by Roger Snortland. (178 pgs.)
$16.95 each in a 6x9" paperback.

Blessed Are The Peacemakers

A rousing tale that traces the heroic Rit Gatlin from his enlistment in the Confederate Army in Little Rock to his tragic loss of a leg in a Kentucky battle, to his return in the Ozarks. He becomes engaged in guerilla warfare with raiders who follow no flag but their own. Rit finds himself involved with a Cherokee warrior, slaves and romance in a land ravaged by war.

Written by Joe W. Smith (444 pgs.)
$19.95 each in a 6 x 9 paperback

Home Front

Read the continuing story of Carrie Amundson, whose life in North Dakota began in *Bonanza Belle*. This is the story of her family, faced with the challenges, sacrifices and hardships of World War II. Everything changed after the Pearl Harbor attack, and ordinary folk all across America, on the home front, pitched in to help in the war effort. Even years after the war's end, the effects of it are still evident in many of the men and women who were called to serve their country.

Written by Elaine Ulness Swenson. (304 pgs.)
$15.95 each in a 6x8-1/4" paperback.

Outward Anxiety - Inner Calm

Steve Crociata is known to many as the Optician to the Stars. He was diagnosed with a baffling form of cancer. The author has processed experiences in ways which uniquely benefit today's readers. We learn valuable lessons on how to cope with distress, how to marvel at God, and how to win at the game of life.

Written by Steve Crociata (334 pgs.)
$19.95 each in a 6 x 9 paperback

Seasons With Our Lord

Original seasonal and special event poems written from the heart. Feel the mood with the tranquil color photos facing each poem. A great coffee table book or gift idea.

Written by Cheryl Lebahn Hegvik. (68 pgs.)
$24.95 each in a 11x8-1/2 paperback.

Pycnogenol®

Pycnogenol® for Superior Health presents exciting new evidence about nature's most powerful antioxidant. Pycnogenol® improves your total health, reduces risk of many diseases, safeguards your arteries, veins and entire circulation system. It protects your skin - giving it a healthier, smoother younger glow. Pycnogenol® also boosts your immune system. Read about it's many other beneficial effects.

Written by Richard A. Passwater, Ph.D. (122 pgs.)
$5.95 each in a 4-1/8 x 6-7/8" paperback.

Remembering Louis L'Amour

Reese Hawkins was a close friend of Louis L'Amour, one of the fastest selling writers of all time. Now Hawkins shares this friendship with L'Amour's legion of fans. Sit with Reese in L'Amour's study where characters were born and stories came to life. Travel with Louis and Reese in the 16 photo pages in this memoir. Learn about L'Amour's lifelong quest for knowledge and his philosophy of life. Written by Reese Hawkins and his daughter Meredith Hawkins Wallin. (178 pgs.)
$16.95 each in a 5-1/2x8" paperback.

Pay Dirt

An absorbing story reveals how a man with the courage to follow his dream found both gold and unexpected adventure and adversity in Interior Alaska, while learning that human nature can be the most unpredictable of all.

Written by Otis Hahn & Alice Vollmar. (168 pgs.)
$15.95 each in a 6x9" paperback.

Spirits of Canyon Creek *Sequel to "Pay Dirt"*

Hahn has a rich stash of true stories about his gold mining experiences. This is a continued successful collaboration of battles on floodwaters, facing bears and the discovery of gold in the Yukon.

Written by Otis Hahn & Alice Vollmar. (138 pgs.)
$15.95 each in a 6x9" paperback.

First The Dream

This story spans ninety years of Anna's life. She finds love, loses it, and finds it once again. A secret that Anna has kept is fully revealed at the end of her life.

Written by Elaine Ulness Swenson.
(326 pgs.)
$15.95 each in a 6x8-1/4" paperback

Bonanza Belle

In 1908, Carrie Amundson left her home to become employed on a bonanza farm. One tragedy after the other befell her and altered her life considerably and she found herself back on the farm.

Written by Elaine Ulness Swenson.
(344 pgs.)
$15.95 each in a 6x8-1/4" paperback.

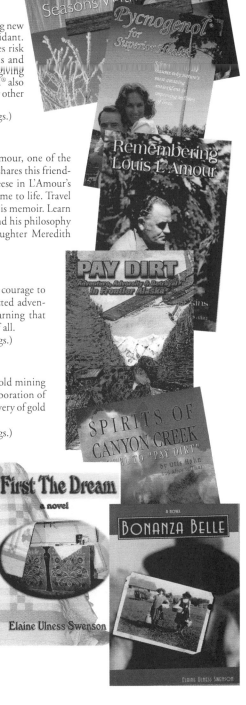

Whispers in the Darkness

In this fast paced, well thought out mystery with a twist of romance, Betty Pearson comes to a slow paced, small town. Little did she know she was following a missing link - what the dilapidated former Beardsley Manor she was drawn to, held for her. With twists and turns, the Manor's secrets are unraveled.
Written by Shirlee Taylor. (88 pgs.)
$14.95 each in a 6x9" paperback.

Dr. Val Farmer's
Honey, I Shrunk The Farm

The first volume in a three part series of Rural Stress Survival Guides discusses the following in seven chapters: Farm Economics; Understanding The Farm Crisis; How To Cope With Hard Times; Families Going Through It Together; Dealing With Debt; Going For Help, Helping Others and Transitions Out of Farming.
Written by Val Farmer. (208 pgs.)
$16.95 each in a 6x9" paperback.

Country-fied

Stories with a sense of humor and love for country and small town people who, like the author, grew up country-fied . . . Country-fied people grow up with a unique awareness of their dependence on the land. They live their lives with dignity, hard work, determination and the ability to laugh at themselves.
Written by Elaine Babcock. (184 pgs.)
$14.95 each in a 6x9" paperback.

Charlie's Gold and Other Frontier Tales

Kamron's first collection of short stories gives you adventure tales about men and women of the west, made up of cowboys, Indians, and settlers.
Written by Kent Kamron. (174 pgs.)
$15.95 each in a 6x9" paperback.

A Time For Justice

This second collection of Kamron's short stories takes off where the first volume left off, satisfying the reader's hunger for more tales of the wide prairie.
Written by Kent Kamron. (182 pgs.)
$16.95 each in a 6x9" paperback.

It Really Happened Here!

Relive the days of farm-to-farm salesmen and hucksters, of ghost ships and locust plagues when you read Ethelyn Pearson's collection of strange but true tales. It captures the spirit of our ancestors in short, easy to read, colorful accounts that will have you yearning for more.
Written by Ethelyn Pearson. (168 pgs.)
$24.95 each in an 8-1/2x11" paperback.

(Add $3.95 shipping & handling for first book, add $2.00 for each additional book ordered.)

Prayers For Parker Cookbook - *Parker Sebens is a 4 year old boy from Milnor, ND, who lost both of his arms in a tragic farm accident on September 18, 2000. He has undergone many surgeries to reattach his arms, but because his arms were damaged so extensively and the infection so fierce, they were unable to save his hands. Parker will face many more surgeries in his future, plus be fitted for protheses.*
This 112 pg. cookbook is a project of the Country Friends Homemakers Club from Parker's community. All profits from the sale of this book will go to the Parker Sebens' Benefit Fund, a fund set up to help with medical-related expenses due to Parker's accident. $8.00 ea. in a 5-1/4"x8-1'4" spiral bound book.